P. 90

Words of Praise for
The Amazing Power of Deliberate Intent
and the Teachings of Abraham

"Masterful teachings from the great masters of the universe!"
— **Dr. Wayne W. Dyer,**
the author of *The Power of Intention*

"My prayer is that everyone, everywhere, reads
The Amazing Power of Deliberate Intent, *a book of pure healing
power and love, written in a practical and accessible style. Abraham's
energy and words will soothe, comfort, guide, and empower you."*
— **Doreen Virtue, Ph.D.,**
the author of *Goddesses & Angels*

*"If there is only one book that you read to positively change the course
of your life, it should be this one. Get out your highlighter and
be prepared to step into the joy of being alive! With wisdom, humor,
and grace, Jerry and Esther Hicks and the teachings of Abraham
show you how to turn life's challenges into personal triumphs.
I love this book and the teachings of Abraham and
can't recommend this book highly enough."*
— **Denise Linn,**
the author of *If I Can Forgive, So Can You*

*"**The Amazing Power of Deliberate Intent** is absolutely fabulous!
I've known Jerry and Esther for many years, and they are the genuine
article. This book can transform every aspect of your life."*
— **Christiane Northrup, M.D.,**
the author of *Mother-Daughter Wisdom*

*"In **The Amazing Power of Deliberate Intent,** Abraham
emphasizes the importance of harnessing the power of our thoughts,
which cannot help but have an effect on all that follows.
This is a fascinating book that I highly recommend to anyone
who is ready to explore the unlimited power of the mind."*
— **Gary Renard,**
the author of *The Disappearance of the Universe*

The Amazing Power of Deliberate Intent

Breath Prachanans

GPBA

IBF

Also by Esther and Jerry Hicks

(The Teachings of Abraham)

Books, Calendar, and Card Deck

Ask and It Is Given

The Teachings of Abraham Well-Being Cards

The Science of Deliberate Creation Daily Planning Calendar/Workbook

A New Beginning I: Handbook for Joyous Survival

A New Beginning II: A Personal Handbook to Enhance Your Life, Liberty, and Pursuit of Happiness

Sara, Book 1: The Foreverness of Friends of a Feather

Sara, Book 2: Sara & Seth: Solomon's Fine Featherless Friends

Sara, Book 3: A Talking Bird Is Worth a Thousand Words

CDs and Audiocassettes

The Amazing Power of Deliberate Intent (Parts I and II)

Ask and It Is Given (Parts I and II)

Introduction to Abraham

Abraham-Hicks Starter Set

Abraham's Greatest Hits

Special Subjects Vol. I & II

A New Adventure (music)

DVDs and Videocassettes

The Art of Allowing

The Science of Deliberate Creation

Relationships & Co-creation

Health & Well-Being

Money & Manifestation

Death & Life

Paranormal Concepts

Transforming Grief

··≡❖≡··

Please visit Hay House USA: **www.hayhouse.com**
Hay House Australia: **www.hayhouse.com.au**
Hay House UK: **www.hayhouse.co.uk**
Hay House South Africa: **orders@psdprom.co.za**

The Amazing Power of Deliberate Intent

Living the *Art of Allowing*

ESTHER AND JERRY HICKS

(The Teachings of Abraham)

HAY HOUSE, INC.

Carlsbad, California
London • Sydney • Johannesburg
Vancouver • Hong Kong

Published and distributed in the United States by: Hay House, Inc., P.O. Box 5100, Carlsbad, CA 92018-5100 • *Phone:* (760) 431-7695 or (800) 654-5126 • *Fax:* (760) 431-6948 or (800) 650-5115 • www.hayhouse.com • *Published and distributed in Australia by:* Hay House Australia Pty. Ltd., 18/36 Ralph St., Alexandria NSW 2015 • *Phone:* 612-9669-4299 • *Fax:* 612-9669-4144 • www.hayhouse.com.au • *Published and distributed in the United Kingdom by:* Hay House UK, Ltd. • Unit 62, Canalot Studios • 222 Kensal Rd., London W10 5BN • *Phone:* 44-20-8962-1230 • *Fax:* 44-20-8962-1239 • www.hayhouse.co.uk • *Published and distributed in the Republic of South Africa by:* Hay House SA (Pty), Ltd., P.O. Box 990, Witkoppen 2068 • *Phone/Fax:* 27-11-706-6612 • orders@psdprom.co.za • *Distributed in Canada by:* Raincoast • 9050 Shaughnessy St., Vancouver, B.C. V6P 6E5 • *Phone:* (604) 323-7100 • *Fax:* (604) 323-2600

Editorial supervision: Jill Kramer • *Design:* Charles McStravick

Library of Congress Cataloging-in-Publication Data

Abraham (Spirit)
The amazing power of deliberate intent : living the art of allowing / [channelled by] Esther and Jerry Hicks.
   p. cm.
ISBN-13: 978-1-4019-0695-5 (hardcover)
ISBN-10: 1-4019-0695-8 (hardcover)
ISBN-13: 978-1-4019-0696-2 (tradepaper)
ISBN-10: 1-4019-0696-6 (tradepaper)
1. Spirit writings. I. Hicks, Esther. II. Hicks, Jerry. III. Title.
BF1301.A168 2006
133.9'3--dc22
                        2005015239

Hardcover: ISBN 13: 978-1-4019-0695-5 • ISBN 10: 1-4019-0695-8
Tradepaper: ISBN 13: 978-1-4019-0696-2 • ISBN 10: 1-4019-0696-6

09 08 07 06   4 3 2 1
1st printing, January 2006

Printed in the United States of America

⸱⸱◦[🖾]◦⸱⸱

This book is dedicated to the long list of teachers who are
enthusiastically sharing our signature book, *Ask and It Is Given,*
with hundreds of thousands of people around the world.
And especially to the amazing array of powerful teachers who
have offered their personal endorsements to our books. . . .
Their willingness to add their highly respected names to our work
has helped make the *Teachings of Abraham* available to those
who are asking for what these works are offering.

⸱⸱◦[🖾]◦⸱⸱

Contents

Foreword

When the Students Are Ready, the Teacher Appears!

by Louise L. Hay,
the best-selling author of *You Can Heal Your Life*

In this mystery called life, we're continually searching for answers. We've always wanted to take control of our lives, but we haven't known how. We've always wanted to alleviate our fears—from the smallest, most intimate ones we have about our bodies and close relationships; to the larger fears we have about death, our government, and the world . . . and even those we may have about life on the outer planets.

This most comforting book takes care of all that. No matter what our fear or concern may be, Abraham not only has an answer for us, but also an easy process that we can do that will take us beyond the fear or the problem to a new level of enjoying life.

I believe that the teachers known as Abraham are some of the best on the planet today. Their words have certainly expanded my own outlook on life. And I'm most grateful to Jerry and Esther Hicks for their time and devotion to bringing these teachings to us at this point in time and space. There is a time and a season to expand our knowledge, and this time is now. And *you* are being blessed and prospered by having this book come into your hands.

I've been aware of Abraham, and of Jerry and Esther Hicks, for several years. The moment I heard Abraham's words, I felt a deep connection. *This is a teacher who's doing very good work,* I thought.

And the more I was exposed to the teachings, the more praise I had for the teacher.

In time I came to know Jerry and Esther. I was most impressed by how well they lived the teachings. Here were two joyous people, manifesting good experiences at every turn. They loved each other and loved life more than most people I know. I enjoyed seeing how they always seemed to communicate with each other with joy and laughter. It does my heart so much good to see people really enjoying life all the time.

We at Hay House are very proud to be the publisher of this series of books, and to have the opportunity to now take this work to a larger worldwide audience. *Ask and It Is Given,* the first book in this series, was called (by best-selling author Wayne Dyer) "a publishing milestone that offers you a blueprint for understanding and implementing your own destiny."

This book, the second in the series, takes you further into yourself. It builds self-confidence, as you'll find that you now have innumerable tools to help you take care of any situation that may come along. As this self-confidence builds, you learn that you can accomplish anything. You'll learn to release struggle, and instead begin practicing the *Art of Allowing.* You'll also be delighted to find out how easy it is to live life as joyously as you always wanted to.

I suggest you do as I do, and keep both books by your bedside for morning and evening reading. You'll sleep better, you'll begin your days by allowing only good to enter your life . . . and you'll feel wonderful as you do so!

— *Louise*

❧❧❧ ❧❧❧

Preface

by Jerry Hicks

Have you ever considered your personal evolution in light of those events that were a major catalyst to your subsequent feeling of fulfillment?

In your album of pleasing memories, have you stored mental pictures of those moments during which you seemed to have been influenced toward becoming, achieving, or manifesting what you really wanted to be, do, or have?

Do you sometimes recall—with surging waves of appreciation—those persons, books, and seemingly chance circumstances that offered you words or experiences that afforded you a fresh spark of philosophical clarity?

Call those brief experiences *turning points;* call them *crossroads;* call them *signposts* on your path; or even *touchstones* to a moment of a particular feeling of Well-Being, perhaps . . . but have you not been aware of their lasting, positive effects on your life?

I began writing this Preface while parked on "our" dirt trail that runs between the French Broad River and the Biltmore Estate's duck pond. My wife, Esther, and I have been presenting workshops here in Asheville, North Carolina, for 15 years now. This spot by the river is one of our favorite places to visit as we participate with the spring goslings and then later the fall migration of thousands of Canada geese as they knowingly wing their way across the skies, while we, too, intersect with the changing seasons here as we loop back and forth across this nation. So here I sit, at the most joyous period of my life doing what brings me so much pleasure. I'm writing this with the intention of offering you some practical reasons to put into practice (so you can deliberately experience more of who you really are) the Teachings of Abraham.

We have been reminded, *Words don't teach; life experience teaches*. And although this is a book of *words*, the powerful ones you're about to read here are going to reveal some uplifting new perspectives to you, which you can now allow to become good-feeling new beliefs. Your new beliefs can—by the natural Laws of the Universe—in turn, generate new and joyous life experiences . . . and from your elevated experiences of joy, you'll discover more of the life-enhancing knowledge that you've been asking for.

I expect that you'll find this book to be one of those treasures you'll forever cherish as a clarifying guide to all you'll ever want to be, do, or have. If the only awareness that I received from this book was the life-changing (for me), in-depth understanding that *you create your own truth*, this book would have served me extremely well. Reading that "truths" are but *beliefs* that have been held for a time, and "beliefs" are but *thoughts* that have been held over a period of time, has truly emphasized my awareness of the amazing power of thought.

Recently, I overheard a highly successful entrepreneur stating (when asked how he was capable of achieving such a stupendous degree of success), "I think big. . . . Since I'm going to be thinking anyway, I decided long ago, *Why not think big?*" This is a demonstration of the amazing power of thought.

Many years ago, I recall reading something written by one of the world's most highly regarded geniuses of the 20th century. He said, in effect: "Most humans are only utilizing less than one percent of their true potential. . . . Ninety-nine percent of their potential to be, do, or have remains forever untapped during their complete lifetime." This book, *The Amazing Power of Deliberate Intent,* will reveal the dynamic processes for using more of your untapped potential—in this lifetime. Have you ever wondered how much potential for joy lies yet untapped within you? At some level of your consciousness, have you ever been aware that, even during your most joyous moments in this life, there's so much more joy that you could experience?

As magnificent as your body has ever felt to you, or performed for you, haven't you somehow known that it could be even better? And when you relive those delicious relationship experiences that you've shared with those whose lives you've touched as you've grown into the Being that is now you—aren't you aware that there must be many more delightful relationships with so many more inspiring persons who are out there waiting for you to attract them into your life experience?

In just a few pages you're going to meet Abraham—"teachers of teachers," they've called themselves. (For those of you who may be new to these teachings, Abraham is referred to in the plural tense because they're a Collective Consciousness.) Abraham has been described by some of the most eminent authors and philosophers in the world as "the greatest teachers on our planet today. . . ." And when I first met Abraham two decades ago, I, too, was drawn to their ability to teach, and what I wanted to learn more about was: *How can I help others to achieve greater financial success?*

I recall (while living in a Volkswagen camper) reading Napoleon Hill's classic book *Think & Grow Rich*, where he said: "When riches begin to come they come so quickly, in such great abundance, that one wonders where they have been hiding during all those years before. . . ."

Think & Grow Rich certainly gave me what I'd been asking for. After discovering that book on a coffee table in a small motel in Montana (and then faithfully utilizing the principles put forth within), my life evolved from earning just enough in the entertainment industry to "not have to go to work" to, in a very few years, building and enjoying a multimillion-dollar distribution business. To anyone who would listen, I constantly gave the credit for my success to the principles I had learned in Hill's book.

The principles worked so well for me that I soon began using *Think & Grow Rich* as a textbook to teach my business associates what I'd been learning. However, after a few years of doing so, I became aware that only a few of my "students" had developed million-dollar businesses. Although there were many who did achieve more-than-modest success, there were some who seemed to achieve almost no financial growth at all no matter how many financial seminars they attended.

After about ten years of that, and after reaching all of my original business goals, I began searching for answers as to how I could more effectively help more people achieve *their* desires . . . and from that "asking," Esther and I were given the avenue to these *Teachings of Abraham.*

There isn't space in this brief Preface to explain in any great detail who, or what, Abraham is, nor how we came to meet them, but if that information is of interest to you, you can experience a free download of a 74-minute recording of *An Introduction to Abraham* by going to our Website at: **www.abraham-hicks.com**— or you can order the CD or cassette from our office: Abraham-Hicks Publications, P.O. Box 690070, San Antonio, TX 78269. Telephone: [830] 755-2299.

Here, however, is an overview of our Abraham experience: Esther and I had been told that by quieting our minds (meditating) for 15 minutes a day, we could receive the answers to what we were asking for, and although Esther did experience some extremely strong physical sensations the first time we meditated together, it wasn't until after nine months of daily meditation that we experienced any meaningful form of intellectual communication. *Intellectual,* in that as Esther's head had begun moving methodically, we discovered that her nose was writing out letters—sort of like spelling out words on an invisible chalkboard in the air: "I AM ABRAHAM. . . ."

To quote Abraham's definition of themselves: *Abraham is not a singular consciousness as you feel that you are in your singular bodies. Abraham is a Collective Consciousness. . . . There is a Non-Physical Stream of Consciousness, and as one of you asks a question, there are many, many points of Consciousness that are funneling through what feels to be the one perspective (because there is, in this case, one human, Esther, who is interpreting or articulating it), so it appears singular to you. . . . We are multidimensional and multifaceted and certainly multi-consciousness. . . .*

I began, immediately, asking questions, and Abraham began answering—at first, by spelling out words using Esther's nose. It later evolved to Esther translating Abraham's Non-Physical blocks of thought into our language through her typewriter, and a few months later, Esther began speaking words for the thoughts she was receiving from Abraham.

A couple of years earlier, I had discovered the *Seth* material (Jane Roberts and Robert Butts had received, in a similar manner, these widely published books). As such, I understood, somewhat, what was happening to us, but as far as we knew, neither of us were asking for, or expecting to receive, the experience for ourselves. I was expecting, and asking for, ways to more effectively teach others how to achieve more successful lives—but not through *this* avenue.

Both Esther and I wanted the wisdom that Abraham was so willing to offer us, but we were both apprehensive as to how something as seemingly strange as this phenomenon would fit into our already well-established business procedures and perspectives. For me, my business principles had to be learnable/teachable. My often-stated intent was that each person whom I touched would be either elevated, or would remain basically where they were when I met them, and it was my intention (and it still is) that no one would ever be diminished as a result of coming into contact with me. For Esther, the principles simply had to prove to feel good when put into practice.

Esther, at first, experienced a more-or-less natural physical resistance to allowing the Abraham experience. For instance, when this "speaking for Abraham" began, she would sit in a chair, eyes tightly closed, hands clenched on the arms of the chair, with her voice projecting from that taut physical posture in a seemingly strident tone.

As the years passed, and as the asking of thousands upon thousands of people continued to evoke Abraham's answers through Esther, her body began to physically relax. First, her eyes opened, then her hands and arms began to gesture; and then a few years later, her body progressed from sitting to standing (braced by a chair or a lectern) to moving gracefully from place to place.

Concurrently, with the relaxing of Esther's body, came the relaxing of her voice. If you were to hear one of our earlier recordings, you would distinguish what you might describe as a foreign accent of some unknown origin. But today, after nearly 20 years of relaxing into speaking for Abraham, the *voice* you would hear would not *sound* very different from Esther's. What you *would* notice as different would be what I would term Abraham's intellectual and attitudinal stances.

One more point before I conclude this Preface: If you've read our previous book, *Ask and It Is Given,* you've already learned that Abraham teaches that we're here having this physical Earth experience for the creative joy of the journey, and that we're not here to try to fix anything or get anything done. Abraham teaches that everything that any one of us ever wants or does is only because we believe that in the achieving of it, we will feel better than we now do . . . and Abraham tells us that there's nothing more important than that we feel good. . . .

So, if we're not here to fix something or to get something done, how can we know if our life on Earth has been a success? Abraham teaches us that success is not measured by the physical things we accomplish or the stuff we gather. They tell us that our success is measured by the degree of joy we're experiencing during our journey through this life.

And so, if you're looking for evidence of someone's success in utilizing the teachings of Abraham, simply pay attention to the amount of joy they're experiencing in the moment, for all that any one of us ever says, does, or attempts to be *(whatever it is!)* is only because we want to reach a state of feeling better.

You may have discovered that wealth, health, relationships, or physical accomplishments aren't what bring you happiness. But you may be amazed to learn that by deliberately finding and maintaining your vibrational balance on your intended pathway of joy, you'll also be attracting whatever you want to be, do, or have—and you can have the happiness, too.

Esther and I have, for two decades now, used the teachings of Abraham to maintain our fun-filled relationship with one another. We've attracted a staff of brilliant, delightful, extremely capable employees and independent contractors who allow the business aspects of the evolution of this philosophy to smoothly flow and grow. We've also attracted spectacular friends and business associates, while not forgoing the joy of the memories of those with whom we no longer personally interact.

Our health is perfect: no doctors (except as friends), no medical examinations, and no medical insurance—yes, physical glitches sometimes occur, but they very shortly resolve themselves as we return to Energy balance. Financially, we paid more taxes last year than the total profits received from all of our years before we learned the principles of deliberate intentions. In other words, it works!

And, above all, I know of no two happier people (with the exception, maybe, of our grandchildren, Laurel, Kevin, and Kate). Esther and I travel this nation presenting *Art of Allowing* workshops to thousands of people in up to 60 cities a year. We drive our "monster bus" (it's a Marathon conversion of a 45-foot-long Prevost tour bus), and printed across the back, in very large friendly letters is: LIFE IS SUPPOSED TO BE FUN.

Perhaps you've felt it, too, but from the time I was five years old I can remember having the desire to somehow help others live happier lives. And so, as my life evolved, I found many varied avenues of expression to perform many versions of that. As I write this for you, I'm feeling such appreciation for those persons (far too many to even consider mentioning here) who have been an influence in my joyous life experience. And although I probably can't credit the *Teachings of Abraham* for actually *attracting* Abraham, I do credit them for the massive physical evolution of this message. I also credit them for the degree of joy that Esther and I experience as we're blessed with this opportunity to create different means of projecting their joy-based philosophy of practical spirituality to you.

— *From my heart, Jerry*

᷂ᷢ ᷂ᷢ ᷂ᷢ ᷂ᷢ ᷂ᷢ ᷂ᷢ

[Please note that since there aren't always physical English words to perfectly express the Non-Physical thoughts that Esther receives, she sometimes forms new combinations of words, as well as using standard words in new ways (for example, capitalizing them when normally they would not be) in order to express new ways of looking at life.]

An Introduction to Abraham

by Esther Hicks

ello, my name is Esther, and I'm the translator of the vibration of Abraham. Abraham has explained to me that I'm able to receive, at an unconscious level of my human Being, their vibrational intent. They tell me that I'm receiving these signals, like those emitted by a radio, at an unconscious level, and then translating them into the word equivalent. They've explained to me that I'm bridging the physical world, in which *I* am focused, with the Non-Physical world in which *they* are focused.

They told me, in the beginning of my receiving of them, that I was a particularly good translator for them because I didn't have strong biases or opinions that would make it difficult for me to receive them clearly. They said that it wasn't so much that I hadn't made up my mind about anything, as it was that I wasn't pushing hard against anything. I was, for the most part, just taking life as it came, and I was in a particularly good vibrational place when I made my first contact with Abraham.

Abraham has explained that everyone has the ability to receive information from the Non-Physical, as I'm doing with Abraham. Just as we all have access to writing beautiful music or painting beautiful pictures, it's all there for all of us to tap in to at any time from any physical vantage point. And just as there's enormous variety in the way people translate music or art—there's enormous variety in the way people interpret Non-Physical Energy. Understanding that, we always document what I translate from Abraham as *Abraham-Hicks* in an effort to distinguish my unique translation from anyone else's.

Abraham suggested to me, in the beginning of my translating for them, that I not read what others have written or what others are writing, for they wanted my interpretation of them (Abraham) to be uncluttered by opinions of others. They didn't want me to worry that I was unconsciously picking up information from other books or people. They wanted me to feel assured that I was, in fact, a pure translator of what they were offering.

Now, all these years later, from time to time I've picked up something or other that someone has sent us, and I can always feel the vibrational compatibility, or lack of it, when I read. Abraham has assured me that at this point I'm in no danger of hindering my ability to hear them accurately when I read, but I can feel that it often takes some time to get myself really tuned in to their pure thought. So, while many people lovingly send us books, manuscripts, or information in a variety of formats, I prefer not to read any of it, for it's my intention to translate as clearly as possible what Abraham is projecting through me.

Abraham has explained to me that thought-by-thought, sentence-by-sentence, discussion-by-discussion, we (Abraham and Esther) have found accurate and unique ways of explaining their teachings that continue to expand and clarify. As they offer a block of thought, I do the best job I can (unconsciously) of finding physical words that most accurately depict their meaning. And when my words and Abraham's meanings match, off we go on some powerful, interesting, and clarifying rampage. And every time that subject is approached, the clarification increases.

What fun this has been for me! I can sense the love, power, and joy that Abraham feels in their process of speaking through me. Nearly every day we receive yet another request from somewhere in the world to present another Abraham-Hicks seminar, and our schedule of events grows a little more every year. However, at this point, it isn't possible to do something more unless we stop doing something we're already doing.

Jerry and I see our work as meeting with as many people as we can (in a question-and-answer format) so that Abraham's message can continue to expand, and there's nothing that we enjoy more than being in a room full of eager *Art of Allowing* workshop attendees who've come to us with their newly refined questions for Abraham.

The questions that people bring to Abraham, as well as those that erupt from our personal lives, are what cause Abraham's message to continue to clarify and expand. And whenever Abraham offers a suggestion of any kind, Jerry and I always do our best to understand it and apply it to our own lives. Over the years, Abraham has offered many processes—they lovingly tell us that they're *eternal spewers of processes.* So whenever they offer one, I always watch for an opportunity in my own life to apply it—and I always receive immediate and satisfying results from my efforts. When I look at the wonderful way we're living, see the amazing results we're experiencing in every area of our lives, feel the security that comes from understanding that we *do* create our own reality, and feel the satisfaction of having created such a wonderful reality, I want everyone to come to know what we've already discovered.

We hold approximately 60 workshops every year, and we drive from city to city in our amazing motor coach that Abraham lovingly refers to as the "monster bus." We continue to find lovely places to park, take our walks, and write our books. For finding a place where we feel wonderful is an important key to relaxing, and to receiving from Abraham. When we're at home in Texas, I have many quiet, private, and beautiful places to choose from where I can sit and receive Abraham's message. But my favorite, always, is our amazing tree house. I always feel happy anticipation of what Abraham will have to say as I climb up into the treetops with my laptop computer and settle into the delicious Energy of Abraham.

--◦[🖼]◦--

As I closed my eyes and relaxed, waiting to begin receiving what I knew would be another wonderful book, Abraham said to me: *Esther, these words will flow easily. So many readers are reading* <u>*Ask and It Is Given,*</u> *and their questions for clarifications are already reaching us. Therefore, writing this book, which is a different book, yet a continuation of the first one, will flow easily for you. Enjoy this process. We are enjoying your enjoyment of your tree house. Now, let us begin. . . .*

∽∽∽ ∾∾∾

Chapter 1

A New Way of Looking at Life

Contrary to what many of our physical friends believe, life on planet Earth is at its all-time best . . . and getting better! This powerful and accurate statement is not only based on our observation of the intricate details of life on Earth, but also on our knowledge of the powerful Laws of the Universe and our understanding that all things are eternally expanding and improving.

People often complain about modern life, stating that it lacks something they remember enjoying in earlier times, and they long to return to those eras or conditions. But we never look to the past for better times, for we understand that what is happening now and what is coming next will always contain the best that life has to offer.

People often misunderstand their role in this magnificent process of Eternal expansion, humbly seeing themselves as insignificant in the larger scheme of things. Some believe that God, or some Higher Power, has created all things, including them, and that now they are here on planet Earth working to achieve a more Godly state, or to achieve God's approval. Others have decided that the world is Godless, and so they, therefore, strive to please no one.

From our broader, Non-Physical vantage point, we understand the power, purpose, and value of the human Being, the human mind, and human thought, for we know that you are the Leading Edge of thought. We understand the value of the variety in which you are living, and the *purpose* of the contrast that you observe. We feel the clarity that arises from your focus in your environment, and we revel in the expansion of thought that results from your exposure to your life experiences. We understand creation—and we understand the power of thought.

You are not here in your physical body striving to achieve the Non-Physical, for you are not separate from the Non-Physical; you are an extension—a Leading Edge extension—of that Non-Physical Energy. You are not here on planet Earth trying to get back to what is Non-Physical, but instead, you are summoning the Non-Physical outward to where *you* are. And in that summoning, *All-That-Is* expands, and your summoning is the reason for the expansion.

Your Every Preference Is Heard and Answered

As you live your life, aware of your environment and all of its contrasting components, a natural process of clarifying your personal preferences occurs. Sometimes these preferences are so fully conscious that you speak of them in terms of your desires, and sometimes they are more subtle and no words are spoken, for these preferences happen at many levels of your Being. Even the cells of your body are points of Consciousness "who" are experiencing contrast and clarifying their preferences. In fact, everything around you: your animals, your trees—even your rocks, dirt, and dust—are actually pulsing, living Consciousnesses who are experiencing contrast and who have preferences. And these living, pulsing preferences have summoning power.

In simpler terms, we like to say: *When you ask, it is given. It is always given. It is given every time. No exceptions. . . . When you or anyone or anything asks, it is given.*

And this simple process of exposure to experience, which causes Consciousness to clarify personal preferences, sets a vibrational summoning into motion that causes the Eternal expansion of the Universe.

When you realize that everything you see around you in your time-space reality is Consciousness, that *every* point of Consciousness is having an experience in which its own preferences are born, and that every preference is heard and answered, then you must understand, as we do, that all is very well.

You Are a Powerful Leading-Edge Creator

You are on the Leading Edge of thought, experience, and expansion. You are certainly not alone in this, for all that has come before you is aware of where you are, what you are doing, and what you are asking for. The Non-Physical aspect of this Leading-Edge you is experiencing the expansion, also, reveling in the new ideas, and joyously joining you as you continue to move into your powerful future.

It is our desire that you remember *all* that you are so that you can enjoy this Leading-Edge vantage point in the way you intended as you decided to come forth into this physical body.

You are not inferior Beings in need of enlightenment. You are not insignificant particles in a vast, unending Universe. You are not misguided or forgotten children trying to find your way home. . . . You are powerful Leading-Edge creators riding the most significant wave of expansion that has ever occurred. And it is our desire that you return to your conscious awareness of this so that your time in this physical body can be one of deliberate, conscious joy!

৺৵৺৵৺৵ ৡৣ৵ ৡৣ৵ ৡৣ৵

Chapter 2

Life on Planet Earth
Continues to Get Better

E ach generation living on your planet benefits from the life experiences of previous generations. We suppose that this statement seems obvious to most who would read it; however, it is a much more powerful statement than most would understand at first glance.

When you contemplate the statement from your awareness of the *Law of Attraction (that which is like unto itself is drawn),* and when you remember that everything that exists in your physical time-space reality exists because of a focused asking from this time-space reality, you begin to get a sense of the importance of all who have been focused, all who have lived contrast, and all who have been asking—asking for answers to questions; resolutions to problems; improvements to situations, and fulfillment of desires.

This living of the contrast, which causes a focusing of desire, calls forth the Creative Energy of the Universe, and is, in fact, what causes all Life to evolve. It would be accurate to say that this living of contrast equals the *asking* or *desire* that summons the Energy that is Life.

There Is Great Satisfaction in Deliberate Creation

We have been speaking often about the Creative Process, and we have been explaining that you are the creator of your own experience. And many are beginning to make the absolute correlation between what they are thinking, how that thought feels, and what then manifests in response to that focus. And as many around the world are becoming students of *Deliberate Creation,* focusing, intentionally, toward specific personal creations, they are finding great satisfaction in doing that.

We enjoy seeing our physical friends deliberately focusing their thoughts while considering the emotional responses to those thoughts—thereby guiding the creation of their own life experiences into more and more pleasing outcomes. There is great satisfaction in doing that.

We enjoy seeing our physical friends living situations not wanted, then deliberately modifying their focus, thereby shifting the way they feel, thereby changing their point of attraction—and thereby receiving different, more satisfying results. There is great satisfaction in doing that.

So, *focusing intentionally* is *deliberate creation,* and there is great satisfaction in *deliberately* creating pleasing outcomes. It is satisfying to change the condition of one's body from sickness to health. It is satisfying to attract and allow more money for the purchase of many satisfying things. It is satisfying to change relationships, to live in new homes, and to drive new vehicles. It is satisfying to have control over all of the physical trappings of one's own life experience. . . .

The <u>Art of Allowing</u> Your Deliberate Intent

Not so long ago, we encouraged Jerry and Esther to change the name of the Abraham-Hicks Seminars from "The Science of Deliberate Creation" to "The Art of Allowing," because Deliberate Creating is about much more than happy outcomes or improved conditions. Deliberate Creating really is about "Allowing" your own personal connection with the Stream of Well-Being and with all that you consider to be good.

While creation is certainly about outcomes, or the manifestation of wanted things, experiences, and conditions, it is really more about the *process* of creation. In other words, it is wonderful to attract and therefore possess a beautiful new vehicle—but life is really about the *process* of doing so.

Life is really about beginning to feel the slight tugging of dissatisfaction with your current vehicle . . . and then feeling the gentle process of clarifying personal preferences regarding something different . . . and then aligning with the idea and details of the desired vehicle . . . and then consciously witnessing the movement of forces and situations to accommodate the acquisition.

Life is really about the ongoing, never-ending refocusing from each new vantage point. Life is always flowing to you and through you, but for you to have *conscious* deliberate awareness of it is the ultimate in truly living.

Accomplishing an end result is manifestation; *consciously* managing and maintaining your vibrational balance is *Deliberate Living.* And it is really what we call living the *Art of Allowing.*

Your Amazing Power of Deliberate Intent

So, this Leading-Edge book is really about understanding the importance of having a *deliberate intent* for an end result, while at the same time, tending to the balance of your Energy along the way. But it is much more about an awareness of the balance of your Energy than it is about goal-setting or focusing on end results. And it is from this very important distinction that this book, *The Amazing Power of Deliberate Intent,* has come forth.

As you come to understand and effectively practice the processes offered here, you will not only achieve your desired goals and outcomes more rapidly, but you will enjoy every single step along the path even *before* the manifestation of your desires. *Living* your life will be an ongoing journey of joy, rather than one of experiencing long dry spells between occasional moments of temporary satisfaction in the achieving of something wanted.

⋅⋅⋅ ⋅⋅⋅

Chapter 3

Death, as Another New Beginning

Most people do not have an accurate sense of who they really are. They are not really sure where they have come from, or where they are going. And, most important, they do not have a sense of why they are here on planet Earth or their reason for being here.

We offer you our awareness of who you are—and how you fit into the larger picture of *All-That-Is*—because we understand how important that perspective can be for you. Once you remember who you are and regain your sense of total continuity of where you have come from and where you are going, your powerful *now* will become infinitely more satisfying.

Perhaps the easiest route to your understanding of the fullness of your Being is for us to begin with a discussion of your physical death. That may seem a bit odd to you if you are one of our physical friends who sees "death" as the "end" of your life experience. However, we do not see what you call your "death" experience as the end of anything, for you are an Eternal Being who has no end.

Just as what you call "death" is not the end of your life experience, what you call "birth" was not the beginning. You are Eternal Consciousness expressing yourself in an endless, glorious dance of Consciousness. You will never cease to be.

When you experience what you call "physical death" (we clarify those words carefully since there is no such thing as *death*), you withdraw your Consciousness from the powerful point of focus that you know as your physical personality, and focus fully into the Non-Physical realm. And in the moment of that change of focus, you leave behind all feelings of inferiority, all doubt, all worry, all hate, all anger and—in a moment in time too short to measure—*you reemerge back into the joyous, pure, Positive Energy perspective that is really who you are.*

When you make a decision to come forth into a physical body, only a part of the Consciousness that is you is temporarily focused into that body. When you experience "physical death," that pointed Consciousness is withdrawn from the physical, and refocused into the Non-Physical.

You Are Here with Deliberate Intent

Focusing Consciousness into a physical body is not something that is taken lightly from your Non-Physical point of view. It is with clear and deliberate intent that you decide to project Consciousness into this time-space reality—and it is with great enthusiasm that you come forth into these bodies. You are filled with eager anticipation for a number of reasons:

- You know that you are an Eternal Being.

- You understand the value of your Being.

- You are fully cognizant of who you are.

- You do not doubt your value or your worthiness.

- You understand that life in this time-space reality is the Leading Edge of thought.

- You know that you are coming into an environment that is stable.

- You know that Well-Being is the dominant order in this environment.

- You know that this is an environment with a tremendous variety of interesting components.

- You understand the Laws of the Universe and the basis of creation.

- You are a master creator, and you know it.

- You like the experience of creating.

- You know that you are good at it.

- You understand and appreciate the *Law of Attraction*.

- You know of its fairness, and you appreciate its consistency.

- You are eager to don your new perspective so that the environment that surrounds you can inspire your new personal preferences and desires.

- You enjoy the sensation of a fresh new desire.

- You understand the Universal response to your fresh new desire.

- You relish the feeling of desire summoning to you and through you.

- You understand that this feeling of desire is the feeling of Life.

- You do not worry about contrast, for you understand its purpose.

- You know that it is through your interaction with contrast and variety that your own desires will be formulated.

- With no reservations whatsoever, you eagerly anticipate the new awareness of desire that is the inevitable result of this Leading-Edge participation in life.

- You come forth not in anticipation of the completion of anything, for you wisely remember the Eternal nature of yourself and of *All-That-Is.*

- You know that life will eternally expand, and that it is not your purpose—or the purpose of anyone— to complete it or finish it.

- You understand that expansion is the natural result of your focus into contrast, because you know that the contrast will cause you to ask.

- You know that when you ask, it is always given; therefore, you have no desire to avoid contrast, because you understand the focusing power of contrast.

- You know that variety and contrast will cause you to determine the specifics of your personal preferences, and you know that each of those preferences, big or small, will be answered in the moment they are born.

And so, an appreciation of your contrasting environment is necessary for you to consciously experience the continuum of who-you-really-are.

You Came Here Expecting to Produce New Desires

We want to help you reclaim the eagerness and the anticipation you felt for this joyous life experience when you entered this physical body and this time-space reality. You did not come forth to fix something that was broken, or to help to redirect a misguided world. You did not come forth to prove your own worthiness, or to earn a reward for efforts offered while here in this body. . . . You came here with full knowledge of your value and worthiness, and with knowledge of the perfection of worlds, physical and Non-Physical—into a contrasting environment that you knew would produce fresh, new personal desires: desires with the power to summon *Energy, Consciousness,* and *All-That-Is* forward into this new Leading-Edge creation.

You knew that you are Life in the process of living Life, in the creation of more Life.

And, most important, you knew (and your Non-Physical part still knows) that the reason for all of all of all of that—is *joy!*

∽∽∽ ∾∾∾

Chapter 4

You Are Vibrational Extensions of the Non-Physical

As you have come to know yourself in your physical body, if you are like most of our physical friends, you do not really know yourself as we know you. You see your physical nature—the flesh, blood, and bone of you, so to speak. And certainly, we acknowledge that you are all of that, but even more than the physical manifestation that you know as your body, we know you as *Consciousness,* as *Vibration,* and as an extension of the *Energy Stream of Source.*

You are far more *Vibration* and *Energy* than you are the physical Being that you recognize as you. And it is only when you understand yourself as a Vibrational Being that you will be able to acknowledge the Vibrational Energy continuum that is really you. And it is really only in the *conscious* realization of that continuum that you will be able to fulfill your true reason for being here in this body, or to truly enjoy yourself in the process.

Often people feel disoriented when they try to see themselves as *Vibration,* or as *Energy,* because they are accustomed to observing only the physical manifestations of those vibrations. In your observation of your world and all of its physical characteristics, it is easy to get so involved in the *results* of the vibrations . . . that you disregard the vibrations that are responsible for those results.

Emotions Indicate Your Non-Physical Relativity

Your physical body was born with such precise and sophisticated vibrational interpreters that you are often unaware that you have them, or that you use them to define your physical reality—but this is a vibrational world, and everything you perceive is because of your ability to interpret vibration:

- Your eyes interpret vibration, and therefore you have the sense of sight.

- Your ears interpret vibration, and therefore you have the sense of hearing.

- Your nose interprets vibration, and therefore you have the sense of smell.

- Your skin interprets vibration, and therefore you have the sense of feeling.

- Your tongue interprets vibration, and therefore you have the sense of taste.

Your ability to understand the continuity of who you are as an Eternal Non-Physical Being (and who you are here in your physical body) comes through the vibrational interpreters that you call <u>emotions.</u>

Your emotions, in every moment, give you an indication of the vibrational relationship between the Non-Physical You and the physical you. Nothing is more important to you than this relationship, and nothing can enhance your physical experience more than an understanding of your emotions, for they tell you everything you need to know about the relationship between the physical you and the Non-Physical You.

Connection, Your Most Natural State of Being

With your deliberate intention and some practice, you will not only have an awareness of your relationship with your Non-Physical Self, but you will be able to maintain a constant vibrational alignment with that Non-Physical Self. We call that conscious state of *deliberate* vibrational alignment with your Source Energy . . . the *Art of Allowing.* It is the art of allowing the fullness of who you are to be present in this powerful Leading-Edge moment.

Whenever you achieve this wonderful Connection, you feel more alive; you feel eagerness, passion, love, appreciation, clarity, vitality, and enthusiasm. In other words, *you allow yourself the benefit of all that you have become, to be present in this Leading-Edge moment of creation.* It is the optimal creative experience; it is the optimal expression of life—and it is your most natural state of being.

So this Connection to who-you-really-are is achieved by vibrational alignment. It is a matching of vibrational signals, so to speak, not so different from what you understand when you tune your radio dial to a special radio frequency to hear music being broadcast from a particular station. You understand that if you want to hear what is being broadcast from 98.7 FM, you must match your tuner/receiver to 98.7 FM. The frequencies must match in order for you to have clear reception.

Although your physical body is not equipped with a dial or a meter that tells you the frequency you are broadcasting, your emotions do provide that equivalent information. *As you pay attention to your emotions, you literally feel your way to your vibrational alignment with your Source.*

☙☙☙ ❧❧❧

Chapter 5

You Came Here to Create
Your Own Experience

Once you make a conscious connection between your physical personality (what you know as *you* here in this body) and the Eternal Non-Physical Consciousness (what is *really You*), you can then get on with the reason you were born into this physical life experience.

An awareness of the continuity of you—an awareness that you did not just begin with this physical birth but that this is but a continuation of who-you-really-are—is vital to living this life experience in anything close to a satisfying, fulfilling way.

Another important component of a satisfying physical life experience is a recognition of your value and your worthiness, and you can achieve that awareness only through an actual Connection with that Non-Physical part of you. In other words, if you do not consciously realize who-you-really-are, and manage to vibrationally align with who-you-really-are, there is no other physical substitute for that Connection.

Some try to fill that feeling of void that is present when they are not vibrationally aligned with their *Non-Physical Inner Being, Consciousness, God, Source,* or *Energy* (there are many different names for this Non-Physical part of you) in a variety of ways: Some seek approval from others, some seek that approval by attempting to modify their behavior in order to conform to rules or guidelines of one group or another, and some work hard to excel in their personal behavior by comparing their behavior to that of others they are observing—but there is no substitute for your vibrational alignment with You.

Vibrational Alignment with Who-You-Really-Are

Nothing is more important than the vibrational alignment, or maintenance of the continuum, between you and You, for your every moment is impacted by your Connection or lack of Connection to your Inner Being—to the Total You that you have become, to the You that you were before you were born into this physical body.

Once you understand who-you-really-are and you consciously work to achieve and maintain your vibrational alignment with who-you-really-are, everything else in your life will fall into wonderful alignment. However, if you do not tend to that Connection, nothing that you can do will fill the void or take the place of that alignment.

Sometimes you are influenced into your alignment by observing something wonderful, or because you are interacting with someone else who is experiencing their own alignment. Sometimes you stumble into your alignment without realizing you are doing it, maybe through your appreciation of something . . . But to have conscious awareness of the value of your alignment, and to understand how to achieve it and how to maintain it, is the optimal life experience. We call that *Deliberate Creation*.

Inner Being and Your <u>Emotional Guidance System</u>

Your awareness of the vibrational variance between what you are vibrationally offering in this moment and the vibrational offering of your *Inner Being* is literally your *Emotional Guidance System*. And when you think of the continuum between you and You, this makes perfect sense.

You are an extension of the *Source Energy You*. And here you are, out here on this Leading Edge of thought, focusing upon some subject. And as you focus your perspective upon the subject, you offer a vibrational frequency, which either matches or does not match the frequency of the way your *Inner Being You* sees it.

For example, let us say that you make a mistake as you are doing your work today. You discover your mistake and you correct it, but then you belittle yourself or feel guilty about your error. You use the making of the mistake as your reason to think unkindly about yourself, and in doing so, you deviate from the loving frequency of the *Inner You, but the Non-Physical part of you* (that *God Force, Source Energy, Inner Being,* or whatever name you assign to that Eternal Non-Physical Energy from which you have come forth) *never, under any conditions, feels anything less than love and appreciation for that which you are.*

Once you learn to recognize the feelings of alignment in relationship to the feelings of misalignment, you can begin to effectively use your *Emotional Guidance System.*

You could say:

I am aligned or misaligned (with the Energy of my Source).

I am connected or not connected (to the Energy of my Source).

I am allowing or resisting (the Energy of my Source).

This conscious awareness of the way you feel is the only consistent, true indicator of your allowing the wholeness of You to be present in this moment. And, although others may inspire or influence you, you cannot count on the influence of any other for your indication of Connection. There are too many other factors—in the lives that *they* are living—for you to depend on them to help you maintain your Connection.

To Feel for Your State of Balanced Energy

Achieving a conscious awareness of your in-this-moment-vibrational-relationship with the vibration of your Source is fundamental to your happy life and to the deliberate creation of your own life. Feeling for the vibrational match between the thoughts you are having in this moment and the thoughts that your Inner Being is having about this moment is what Deliberate Connection really is; and when you are able to consciously *feel* the vibrational discord, or alignment, between those two vibrational vantage points, you will be in conscious awareness of your own *Emotional Guidance System.*

Deliberately reaching for thoughts that cause your two vibrational vantage points to align is the true meaning of the *Balancing of Energy.* When you line you up with You, you experience the balancing of your own Energy, and you come into alignment with the true power of your Being. There is no substitute for this alignment.

From your state of *balanced energy,* you experience clarity, vitality, eagerness, physical wellness, abundance in all things you consider to be good, and an exuberant state of joy. *This is the natural state of who-you-really-are.*

≈§ ≈§ ≈§ ≈§ ≈§ ≈§

Chapter 6

The Attractive Power of Your Creative Thought

Although you may not yet be completely aware of your vibrational nature, you *are* a Vibrational Being living in a Vibrational Universe. In fact, everything is vibrational!

As you give your attention to something: an idea, a memory, a situation you are observing, a dream or fantasy that you are visualizing . . . you are actually activating vibration. And as your focus causes that activation, that vibrational content now becomes your point of attraction. *Whenever you think about anything, its vibrational content becomes an active part of your vibrational essence—and the subject of your attention begins to move toward you.*

Most people do not realize that thinking about something is inviting the essence of that "something" into their experience. Of course, when you made the decision to come forth into this body, you understood the vibrational nature of your world, and of this Universe, and you were enthusiastic about it, for you believed in your ability to deliberately focus.

Knowledge of the vibrational nature of your Universe is both comforting and exhilarating: *comforting,* in the sense that you know that you have nothing to fear because nothing can come to you without your invitation of it; and *exhilarating,* in the sense that you know that you can draw anything that you desire close to you for your joyful experiencing of it.

When you realize that you are the vibrational attractor of all things that come to you and that you do have control of what comes, your world opens to new horizons. . . . There is no need to limit your experience in a guarded or protective stance, for no unwanted thing can force or assert itself into your experience. *You are the creator of your own experience, and no one else has power within your experience. And that is true for everyone.*

The Powerful, Universal <u>Law of Attraction</u>

In the same way that the law of gravity consistently responds to all of the *physical matter* of your planet, the *Law of Attraction* consistently responds to all *vibrations*. Every projection of thought, whether you are focused into the past, present, or future, is vibration and has attraction power. Each thought offers a signal, similar to a radio signal, that the *Law of Attraction* recognizes and matches. This powerful, consistent *Law of Attraction (that which is like unto itself is drawn)* offers consistent results in response to the vibrations that you offer. There are no arbitrary, inconsistent responses that would make the *Law of Attraction* impossible to understand. It is consistent; it is fair; it is always responsive; it is powerful—it is a Deliberate Creator's best friend. Your awareness of the powerful consistency of the *Law of Attraction*—and your understanding of how it works coupled with the *conscious* utilization of your *Emotional Guidance System*—puts you in the powerful position of creating a wonderful, joyous life.

Choosing your objects of attention deliberately, and refining the specifics of your focus by utilizing your *Emotional Guidance System,* renders you a powerful Deliberate Creator who is fulfilling your intention for this physical life experience—for you are now allowing the perspective of your Source to be present in this Leading-Edge experience as you ride the glorious wave of taking thought beyond that which it has been before.

Yours Is a Unique and Personal Life Experience

Although you may know others who seem to be having similar experiences, you are living a unique life experience. In other words, as you move about your world interacting with the components of your time-space reality, experiencing the variety and contrast that surrounds you, you automatically and constantly clarify personal preferences. And as you stand in your unique Leading-Edge perspective, your unique preferences and desires are erupting within you and causing vibrational signals to emanate from you. And as those vibrations, through the *Law of Attraction,* summon vibrational matches unto themselves, everything that you are—and everything that your Inner Being or Source is—experiences the expansion of that summoning.

The Non-Physical part of you revels in the exhilaration of this groundbreaking expansion, for there is no more joyous place in all of existence to be than on this Leading-Edge place experiencing this new awareness firsthand.

We write this book because it is our desire that you experience, firsthand, the joy of this Leading-Edge perspective. We want you to experience the exhilaration of standing on the Leading Edge of thought, fully conscious of the speed of life flowing through you. . . .

Future generations will benefit from the desires that are now emanating from you and from their subsequent attraction power—but it is our desire that you receive the benefit of them, too. Right here, right now!

ॐ ॐ ॐ ॐ ॐ ॐ

Chapter 7

You Are Manifesting the Essence of What You Are Thinking About

When you begin to understand the vibrational nature of thought and the way the *Law of Attraction* responds to it, you then begin to understand how it is that you are the creator of your own reality. Everything about your life is coming to you in response to the focus of your thoughts, but until you understand the vibrational nature of your thoughts and discover a comparative way of recognizing them, you have no *deliberate* control over your own experience.

Deliberate creation is much more than just deliberately choosing a subject of attention and focusing upon it. For while it is a good thing to deliberately choose the subject of your attention, you must *also* feel for the vibrational content of your thought in order to really be in deliberate control of your creating. For example, you may be focused upon the *subject* of financial abundance. But this subject, like all subjects, has great variety within it. On one extreme of the subject is the thought of the *presence* of financial abundance, while on the other extreme of the subject is the thought of the *absence* of financial abundance. *And so, in a simplistic sense, every subject could be seen as two subjects: what is wanted and the lack of what is wanted.*

Each Subject Has a Varied Vibrational Range

When we say to our physical friends, "You get what you think about," sometimes they feel confusion, for they believe that they have been "thinking about" achieving *more money,* a *healthier body,* a *better relationship,* or *more satisfying work.*

People will sometimes argue that they have been definitely thinking about more money, and they do not understand why (if what we say is true) more money is not coming into their experience. But the subject of money has a varied vibrational range. The subject of money ranges from a magnificent, ever-flowing abundance all the way to the desperate absence of abundance. So, merely focusing upon the subject, or the idea, of money is but the beginning of the necessary focusing, or molding of the Vibrational Energy, required to bring money into your experience.

Directing your thought to the *subject* of money is a good first step, but then it is necessary to understand where, on this wide range of vibrational possibilities relative to the subject of money, you actually are. Which end of this vibrational range are you leaning toward? Are you a closer match to the magnificent abundance, or are you a closer match to the desperate absence of abundance? You can easily answer this question when you understand your emotions, for it is through emotional awareness that you understand the vibrational content of your thoughts. The way you *feel* as you are focusing thought is really what matters most.

How Does the Thought Feel to You?

Some are beginning to acknowledge: *You get what you think about.* But we would like to clarify that statement further by saying: *You get what you feel about what you think about.*

So where are you on the sliding scale of possible vibrations relative to the subject of money? You may often say that you want more money, but if you consistently feel disappointment, or even fear, about not having enough money, then your vibrational offering regarding money does not match your statement of desire. And wherever your vibrational offering is, is where your point of attraction is. *What is actually happening in your experience relative to the subject of money always matches the essence of your vibrational offering.*

Observing what is manifesting, or happening to you, can give you an accurate reading of where you are on the Vibrational Scale of possibilities. And that awareness can be extremely helpful. But it is possible for you to be aware of where you are on the Vibrational Scale *before* things manifest, or occur, in your experience, and that is a much more satisfying way to approach the deliberate control of your life experience.

It Is Never Too Late to Change Direction

You can either be aware of your point of attraction post-manifestation (after it happens) or pre-manifestation (before it happens). Of course, we encourage having conscious awareness at all times about the direction you are headed. It would be like traveling in your vehicle, having a particular destination in mind, being on the wrong road altogether and traveling in the opposite direction of your desired destination, but having no awareness that you were going in the wrong direction until you arrived at the wrong place. *You can always correct your course, but the sooner you are aware that you are off your path, the better and more satisfying your journey will be.*

The key to joyful deliberate creating is to choose the subjects of your thoughts *intentionally* while paying close attention to how each thought feels, for unless you are aware of how the thought feels, you have no understanding of where you are on the sliding scale of vibrational possibilities.

ఆ ఆ ఆ ఏ ఏ ఏ

Chapter 8

When You Ask, It Is Always Given

When you made the decision to come forth into this physical body in this time-space reality, you understood the unlimited abundance of this environment. You felt no competition whatsoever from those with whom you would share this planet, for you understood fully that your environment is capable of expanding in proportion to the desires that are born from the exposure to it. You reveled in the idea of interacting with many others; and experiencing a diverse spectrum of intentions, ideas, beliefs, and desires. You understood the value of the vast variety and contrast, for you knew that it would stimulate your thought; you knew that it is only from exposure to contrast that any preferences or desires can be born. And you well understood the value of giving birth to desires, for you understood the summoning power of desires. You knew that whenever you ask, it is always given—without exception.

Let's consider this from a vibrational standpoint: You have an awareness of your environment, which stimulates your own personal preferences. Those preferences, whether you speak them out loud or not, cause you to offer a vibrational emanation (an asking), and the powerful *Law of Attraction* answers your vibrational emanation with other vibrational offerings that match them.

You Launched a Rocket of Desire, but . . . ?

It seems simple enough: *Contrast produces desire; all desire is answered.* . . . So if this is correct, then anyone who desires anything should be the swift receiver of that desire. So how can it be that you could have the *desire* for more money or an improved bodily condition and not get it?

The answer to this often-asked question lies in your awareness of your *Vibrational Sliding Scale.* An intense situation could cause the launching of a powerful desire. And in the moment of the launching of that desire, you are, for that brief time, a vibrational match to it. In fact, it is usually such a brief time of vibrational alignment that we call it a *Rocket of Desire.* But if, over time, you have often been offering thoughts that have registered somewhere else on the Vibrational Scale, then you have most likely practiced yourself into a pattern, or habit, of thought that is quite different from what you are now asking for.

Whenever you think a thought, you activate that thought vibration within you. Whenever a vibration is activated, other thoughts that match it come to it, making it easier and easier for you to think that thought. As you often return your focus to that activated thought, it becomes a *dominant activated thought,* or a *belief.* (A belief is really only a thought that you keep thinking.) And of course, the *Law of Attraction* makes it easy for you to continue to think the thought, because your focus upon it, and the subsequent activation of the vibration of it, cause the *Law of Attraction* to bring to you more thoughts like it—and therefore more evidence of it.

ఆఆఆ ಕಿಕಿಕಿ

Chapter 9

Truth Is All About Your Focus

You may now more fully comprehend that you are a Vibrational Being, and that you *do* create your own reality. Furthermore, you are now coming to understand that you create your own reality through the focus of your thoughts, because your thoughts are vibrations and the *Law of Attraction* responds to those vibrations. Therefore, anytime you are focusing upon anything—past, present, or future—you are in the process of creation.

When your attention is focused upon something that you are observing in your present moment; something you are considering, pondering, or remembering from your past; something you are explaining; or something you are imagining or fantasizing, you are offering a vibration . . . and the *Law of Attraction* is responding to that vibration. And each time you revisit that subject, the process of attracting other vibrations of the same frequency increases, so your signal about that subject gets stronger.

The more you focus upon a subject, the more active that vibration is, and the more of that which is a vibrational match to it is attracted to it. Eventually you will begin to see physical evidence showing up in your experience that matches the essence of the way you have been feeling about the subject.

You Are the Creator of Your Own Truth

As you consider any idea, you activate a vibration about it, and the *Law of Attraction* then offers you other ideas that have the same vibrational frequency. As you continue to ponder the subject, more thoughts that match those thoughts come to you; and as the activation of this idea continues, it becomes stronger, and the attraction power of the idea increases. In time, things will begin to occur in your life experience that match those ideas. Usually at that point, you call the experience *factual* or *truthful.* And no one could deny that it is factual or truthful, for the physical evidence is right there before you, supporting it. But instead of calling it *truth* or *fact,* we call it *creation;* we call it the natural Universal response to your consistently activated vibration. . . . There is no value in focusing upon unwanted things (causing an activation of the vibration within you) that the *Law of Attraction* will respond to, and therefore creating in your reality something you do not want.

Often people will explain that their rationale for giving their attention to a subject is because the subject is *true.* But although there are many subjects that are true that you *would* like to personally experience, there are also many subjects that are true that you would *not* like to personally experience.

It is not important whether it is true or not, but whether or not you want to experience the truth of it in your experience. Anything focused upon long enough must become truth! It is law!

 торе торе торе торе торе торе

Chapter 10

Awareness, as Your Key to Deliberate Creation

Your thriving will be immediately enhanced in the moment you understand and begin to utilize your own *Emotional Guidance System.*

Through your continual exposure to life experience, you are stimulated to constant awareness, which means that you are focusing upon something all day, every day, and that focus is causing an activation of vibration within you. Most people do not realize that they are Vibrational Beings living in a Vibrational Universe, and most are not aware that they are vibrationally attracting their own reality. And so, most people make little or no effort to deliberately focus thought.

In this fast-paced environment, with so much to consider, it would be no small task to have conscious awareness of *every* thought. In fact, a sifting and sorting of all of this data is not possible. Fortunately, you do not have to sort the plethora of thoughts that are moving through you, for the *Law of Attraction* will tend to that sorting process.

Everyone and everything in the Universe is Consciousness. And all Consciousness is Vibration, or Energy. And all Consciousness has the ability to focus (even the one-celled amoeba). All Consciousness is having experience, and all Consciousness is having personal perception of that experience—and constant preferences are being born from that personal perception.

Exposure to the contrast and variety of life causes continual personal preferences to emanate from every point of Consciousness. When exposure to your experiences causes you to give birth to a personal preference (or desire), a vibration emanates from you (a rocket of desire), and your *Inner Being,* your *Source, All-That-Is* begins to immediately respond to that request. In other words, when you ask (from any level of your Being), it is given, every time.

Can You Vibrationally Match Your New Desires?

So the Non-Physical part of you receives your *request,* has keen awareness of your rocket of desire, and turns its undivided attention toward the desire to which you have just given birth. In other words, your *Inner Being* instantly becomes a vibrational match to your new desire—and therefore it immediately receives the benefit of your Leading-Edge launching of your Leading-Edge desire. You, however, from your physical standpoint, are usually not yet a perfect vibrational match to your new desire, for your desire was born from contrast, and so you still have a mix of vibrations within you relative to your desire.

In the moment the new desire or preference has been launched, there was an immediate discrepancy in the vibration of your *Inner Being* or *Source* (who immediately aligned with your new desire), and your personal physical perspective (which still holds a mix of vibrations). Your work now is to activate within your vibration only those aspects that match your new desire. And that is where your *Emotional Guidance System* comes in, for your emotions are your indicators of vibrational alignment or discord.

For example, you are having a conversation with someone who is very busy and does not really want to take the time to have a discussion with you. This person is abrupt with you, even rude. This experience causes a preference to emanate from you. And even if you cannot, or do not, put words to it, the fact is that you prefer to be treated with more respect. And so, a newly defined preference now radiates from you, and your Inner Being finds immediate alignment with the idea of your being treated with more respect. You, however, have not yet found that alignment. You are still recalling this person's attitude, rude words, and actions. Your vibrations are a mixture of how you want to be treated and how you just were treated. You are not a match to your new desire—but your Inner Being is.

If you are sensitive to the way you feel, you can sense the discord between the vibration of your Inner Being and your in-this-moment vibration. In fact, that is what your emotions always indicate: *A good-feeling emotion indicates vibrational alignment between the perspective of your Inner Being and you. A bad-feeling emotion indicates vibrational misalignment between your Inner Being and you.*

Another example: In sorting through your mail, you find several requests for payments of bills due, and as you add them up, you realize that you do not have enough money to pay everything you now owe. In that moment, a desire for more money emanates from you, and your Inner Being focuses surely and immediately upon the idea of more money, and takes pleasure from the idea of this. You, however, continue to sift through your stack of bills, facing the reality of where you now stand. "I have more bills than I have money to pay them," you complain. You have not found alignment with your new desire, and the negative emotion that you feel (worry, anger, frustration) indicates your misalignment with your Source.

No desire, no matter what the subject, can manifest into your experience as long as there is a vibrational difference between the desire and your practiced vibration. You have to practice yourself into vibrational alignment with your desires before they will be realized in your experience.

That's the reason that we refer to your emotions as your *Emotional Guidance System,* for they help you recognize the relationship between the vibration of your desire and the vibration of your offering. No other factors need be considered in the achievement of anything that you want: What others think, what they have lived, what they are living, what you have lived in the past, even what you are living right now—none of that has any bearing whatsoever on your ability to achieve the object of your desires. Only the vibrational relativity between your desire and you is relevant.

ঙ্গ ঙ্গ ঙ্গ ঌ ঌ ঌ

Chapter 11

Vibrational Relativity and Energy Balance

The vibrational relationship between you and your Source is the basis of your *Emotional Guidance System*. Your guidance system, like all guidance, is based upon something in relationship to something else.

Consider the (GPS) navigational system in your vehicle. While it does have the facility to pinpoint your precise location, it is of no value to you in terms of guidance until you enter, or program in, your desired destination. But once the navigational system has that information, it can begin to calculate a proposed route from where you currently are to where you want to go. In the same way, the relationship between your current and desired body weight is the basis of the emotional guidance you receive. The relationship between your current financial situation and the amount of cash you would like to have in your bank account is the basis of the emotional guidance that you receive.

The relationship between where you are and where you want to be is the basis of your personal guidance system. Even without an electronic navigational system, you understand the relativity between where you are and where you want to be, and without that information you could not proceed with any clarity upon your journey. . . . You would just be moving from place to place.

Vibrational Relativity exists in every possible subject: those of great importance, those of lesser importance, those that come up many times in every day, and those that you think about only occasionally. Helpful and precise guidance is readily available to you regarding all things, for there is no subject in your life in which *Vibrational Relativity* is missing.

The Best Path to Your Intended Destinations?

If you have ever utilized an electronic navigational system in your vehicle, you have surely had the experience of programming an intended destination and then, for some reason, deviating from the route. Something along the way may have attracted your attention, so you made an unscheduled turn along your route. . . . Immediately, your navigational system begins signaling you that you are off of your course. You can explain your reasons for departing from your route, but your navigational system will simply continue to tell you that you have deviated from your intended route, because as far as your guidance system is concerned, you *are* off your path. Of course, you could reprogram the system because of your new decision, and your guidance system would then regroup and make a new plan, but as long as you are holding a specific intention of where you want to go but are moving in a different direction from that intention, warning bells will ring.

Now you might say, "But Abraham, surely there is more than one path that will lead to my desired destination." And we agree with you: There are many paths, many satisfying paths, paths that are satisfying for different reasons, which will lead to your desired destination. In fact, the joy of life is really in the journey. However, your vehicle's navigational system is considering the information within its unique system. It has determined where you are, and contained within its information system are many possible routes or paths. So considering all of those factors, your navigational system gives you the best route that it can conclude. In other words, it cannot make decisions or give guidance outside of the information contained in its system.

You Have a Personal *Emotional Guidance System*

Your personal *Emotional Guidance System* operates in a similar way to an electronic guidance system. You cannot receive guidance outside of the routes (or beliefs) contained within your system. Your *Emotional Guidance System of Relativity* is based only upon your *active* vibrations (beliefs) and their relationship with your desired destination. (Remember, a *belief* is really only a *thought* that you keep thinking.)

Your emotions are your indicators of the vibrational relationship of the active vibrations within you. You have come forth into this physical body as an extension of Source Energy, and the vibration of your Source is always an active vibration within you. As you explore the variety and contrast of your own life experience, natural preferences relating to the way you would like things to be are vibrationally emitted from you in the form of vibrational signals (similar to electronic signals). You are literally beaming these signals forward into your future experience.

Whenever a preference or desire is born within you as a result of something that you are living, that vibrational signal shoots forth like a rocket of desire and begins amassing power and clarity in your vibrational future, in what we lovingly refer to as your *vibrational escrow*. It is held there expressly for you. No one else can swoop in and take it, depriving you of your own creation. It remains there, pulsing—gaining power, momentum, and clarification—as you continue to amend your desires through processing more contrasting experiences. *The contrast in which you are focused provides a wonderful basis for the launching of your unique desires, for whenever you are experiencing something that you do not want, you always understand more clearly what it is that you do want.*

Your Source Immediately Joins Your Every Desire

As you are focused here in this time-space reality, viewing life from your unique perspective, you unceasingly emit new signals for the improvement of your own life experience. *In the moment your rockets of desire emanate from you, Source Energy becomes one with those desires. In fact, that is precisely the reason that we continue to unequivocally state to you that when you ask, it is always given, for Source Energy acknowledges your desire, agrees with your desire, knows your desire, and flows with your desire. . . .* The power of your Source immediately becomes one with your desire. And now, the vibrational relativity between your newly launched *desire*—which has been joined by the Energy of Source—and your current habitual thoughts or *beliefs* upon the same subject, become apparent. You can literally feel the agreement or lack thereof between the frequencies of these Energies.

If you collected your bills from your mailbox and realized that you did not have enough money to pay all of them, a *desire* for money would shoot out from you into your vibrational future. And in the moment of that launching, Source Energy would flow with your rocket of desire. But if you continued to agonize over the lack of money in your bank account to pay those bills, your vibration would be very different from that of your desire, and so the emotion of worry, or fear, would be your indication of your vibrational discord.

If someone you love has treated you badly, a rocket of desire to be treated with more respect would shoot from you, and your Source would agree with and respond to your request. . . . Your Source literally forms a vibrational bond with your request or desire, and your request is immediately granted. Source flows with your desire and sees it as you have requested that it be, but if you continue to remember or focus upon the hurtful experience, you hold yourself vibrationally apart from your own request; there is vibrational discord between the vibration of your desire and the vibration of what you are offering as you focus upon your mistreatment.

If the vibration of *what-is* is the dominant vibration within you regarding the subject of your relationship, then your relationship cannot improve. And the emotional pain that you feel is your indication that the vibrational relativity between where you are right now and what you desire must be improved. You must find a way of offering a vibration that matches that of your desire and of your Source if you are to allow yourself to receive the benefit of your own request.

◦ξ ◦ξ ◦ξ ξ◦ ξ◦ ξ◦

Chapter 12

Finding Alignment with Your Source Energy

As you are focused here within your physical body, you are an extension of Non-Physical Source Energy. *The Eternal You is focused here in this physical body. The clear-minded, joyous Being that is the Total of all that you are, flows to you and through you in this body—but your Inner Being, or Source, does not think for you. You are not a puppet doing the bidding of that Broader Self. You are a fully conscious creator expressing your unique desires here in this physical time-space reality. You are free to choose the direction of your own thoughts.*

So, your *Emotional Guidance System* exists to help you to determine, moment by moment, the relationship between the vibration of what you are giving your attention to right now, and the *perspective* of your Inner Being.

As you have been focused here in your physical body, interacting with others and living the details of your own life experience, you have encountered much contrast and variety that has caused many rockets of desire to be launched. You could say that these desires are waiting somewhere in your future experience to be realized by you. We like to say that they are being held, and tended to, for you by Source Energy in a sort of vibrational escrow. They are your creation, they belong to you, and they are simply awaiting your vibrational alignment with them. *And now you must feel your way to that alignment.*

Your *Emotional Guidance System* (the way you feel) is your constant indicator of the vibrational alignment between your active or dominant vibrations (beliefs) and the desires that you have launched that are waiting to be realized or manifested into your life experience. *As you focus upon the subject of your desire, you can feel your harmony or discord: The better you feel, the more in alignment you are with your desire. The worse you feel, the more out of alignment you are with your desire.*

Increased Attention Enhances the Emotional Intensity

As the subject of your desire is activated within you by your attention to it, you can feel where you are on the sliding scale of vibrations. You can sense whether you are leaning toward the abundance of your desire or the lack of abundance of your desire. *Your emotions indicate your current beliefs in relationship with your current desire.*

If your life experience has caused you to launch many rockets of desire relative to a subject, then Source Energy is flowing in a stronger way toward that particular desire. If that is the case, then the emotions that you feel will be stronger regarding that subject. The more attention you give, the more the *Law of Attraction* responds, the faster the Energy moves, and you recognize the feeling of Energy moving faster via those emotions that you describe as enthusiasm, passion, exuberance, or joy.

But what is happening to you when you are feeling the stronger negative emotion of anger, hatred, or fear? Those strong emotions certainly indicate, also, that Energy is moving quickly. (In other words, your contrasting experience has caused you to launch powerful rockets of desire, and Source Energy is now flowing toward those desires.) But the negative emotions that you are feeling are because of the vibrational relativity between your active desire (which has the full attention of your Source) and your active in-the-moment vibration (where *your* attention is right now).

Is Your Focus Predominantly on What You Want?

So, your *Emotional Guidance System* is giving you feedback based on two significant factors: *One,* the power of your desire (or the vibrational speed of your desire) caused by the amount of contrasting experiences and the number of rockets of desires that have been launched about them; and *two,* the direction of your focus right now. In other words, your *Emotional Guidance System* is giving you powerful and accurate guidance regarding the vibrational relationship between where you are right now and where you want to be.

If your life experience has caused you to come to the point where you really want something, and in any given moment, you are focused upon the opposite of that desire, you will feel strong *negative* emotion. But if your desire is strong and your current thoughts are in vibrational alignment with that desire, then you will feel strong *positive* emotion. Your emotions are accurate indicators of the vibrational relativity between where you want to be and where you are right now, and your *Emotional Guidance System* is always accurate and available to you at all times. It is a very good system, indeed.

⋖⋗⋖⋗⋖⋗ ⋗⋖⋗⋖⋗⋖

Chapter 13

Vibrational Relativity Regarding
My Physical Body

The following are some examples of the vibrational relativity between the common *desires* and *beliefs* that we see in many people regarding their physical bodies. First we will state a common *desire* that many people hold regarding their physical body, and then we will list a series of common *beliefs* about that desire. And next, in brackets, following those beliefs, we will indicate the degree of vibrational compatibility between the *desires* and the *beliefs.*

For any desire to be realized by you, or before anything can manifest in your life experience, there must be vibrational compatibility between your desires and your beliefs.

As you read down each of the following lists, notice the feeling of the lessening of resistance—or the improvement in the vibrational relationship—between the stated *desire* and the commonly associated *belief.*

Desire: *I want to live a long, healthy life in this body.*

Belief: It's unlikely that I'll live a long, healthy life because there are many deadly diseases in my family history. [This belief is vibrationally incompatible with the stated desire.]

Belief: I was born in times that were very different from my parents, their parents, and *their* parents. [This belief is vibrationally more compatible with the stated desire.]

Belief: Today I have greater access to food and information to assist me in maintaining better health. [This belief is even more vibrationally compatible with the stated desire.]

Desire: *I want to live a long, healthy life in this body.*

Belief: My parents were not healthy people. [This belief is vibrationally incompatible with the stated desire.]

Belief: My parents and I lead very different lives. Our environments are different, what we eat is different, and how we see ourselves is different. [This belief is vibrationally more compatible with the stated desire.]

Belief: There is no relationship between my parents' health and my own. [This belief is even more vibrationally compatible with the stated desire.]

Desire: *I want to live a long, healthy life in this body.*

Belief: There are many diseases present in our society today. [This belief is vibrationally incompatible with the stated desire.]

Belief: I have long been surrounded by many diseases and possibilities of diseases that I haven't contracted. [This belief is vibrationally more compatible with the stated desire.]

Belief: The existence of a disease doesn't mean that I'm personally susceptible. [This belief is vibrationally somewhat more compatible with the stated desire.]

Belief: My intelligent body has often come into contact with diseases that it has comfortably dealt with without my conscious awareness. [This belief is even more vibrationally compatible with the stated desire.]

Desire: *I want to live a long, healthy life in this body.*

Belief: Even though new cures to diseases are discovered, new diseases continue to pop up. [This belief is vibrationally incompatible with the stated desire.]

Belief: The standard of physical health continues to rise worldwide. [This belief is vibrationally more compatible with the stated desire.]

Belief: Diseases that thrive in the *absence* of vibrational alignment cannot affect someone who is *in* vibrational alignment. [This belief is somewhat more vibrationally compatible with the stated desire.]

Belief: Another's resistance to *their* Well-Being has nothing to do with me and *my* Well-Being. [This belief is even more vibrationally compatible with the stated desire.]

Desire: *I want to live a long, healthy life in this body.*

Belief: Most people eventually experience physical decline. [This belief is vibrationally incompatible with the stated desire.]

Belief: Different people experience different degrees of physical decline. It's not necessary to be sick at the end of one's physical life. [This belief is vibrationally more compatible with the stated desire.]

> *Belief:* The length of time in one's physical body and the degree of decline aren't related. [This belief is even more vibrationally compatible with the stated desire.]

Desire: *I want to be active and strong all of my physical life.*

Belief: As I get older in my physical body, it's inevitable that my physical strength and endurance will diminish. [This belief is vibrationally incompatible with the stated desire.]

> *Belief:* When I observe people who are experiencing a physical decline, I don't know the details of their life experience. [This belief is vibrationally more compatible with the stated desire.]

> *Belief:* There are strong people at all ages and weak people at all ages; age is not the determining factor. [This belief is even more vibrationally compatible with the stated desire.]

Desire: *I want to achieve and maintain a healthy, attractive body weight.*

Belief: It's very difficult to maintain the body weight I desire without doing strenuous daily exercise and depriving myself of things I want to eat. [This belief is vibrationally incompatible with the stated desire.]

> *Belief:* As I observe others, there's a great variety in their activity and food consumption, causing a great variety of results. [This belief is vibrationally more compatible with the stated desire.]

> *Belief:* It's possible for me to find a comfortable lifestyle that will give me the results I want. [This belief is even more vibrationally compatible with the stated desire.]

Desire: *I want to be agile and flexible.*
I want my body to move easily and to feel good while it moves.

Belief: As I get older, I become stiff, brittle, and less flexible. [This belief is vibrationally incompatible with the stated desire.]

Belief: There are many good-feeling, flexible older people and many not-good-feeling, inflexible younger people. Age is not the determining factor. [This belief is vibrationally more compatible with the stated desire.]

Belief: I notice that when I decide to move my body deliberately on a daily basis, the condition of my body steadily improves—at any time, and every time! [This belief is even more vibrationally compatible with the stated desire.]

Desire: *I want clarity of thought.*
I want to learn easily and to retain what I've learned.

Belief: I'm often confused and don't retain the things I read or learn. [This belief is vibrationally incompatible with the stated desire.]

Belief: I've noticed that my memory is good when I'm dealing with a subject I'm interested in. [This belief is vibrationally more compatible with the stated desire.]

Belief: When I want clarity, and when I deliberately focus, I'm clear. [This belief is even more vibrationally compatible with the stated desire.]

Desire: *I want clarity of mind.*
I want to remember where I put things.

Belief: I can't remember where I put things. [This belief is vibrationally incompatible with the stated desire.]

Belief: Even when I can't remember where I've put something, in time, I always find it again. [This belief is vibrationally more compatible with the stated desire.]

> *Belief:* If I make a decision about the best place to put something and I think about why this is a good place to put it, I then easily remember that I've put it there. [This belief is even more vibrationally compatible with the stated desire.]

You have undoubtedly come to many opinions or beliefs about many things. You may have seen some of what you believe reflected in the examples that you have just read. But the all-important question that you must ask yourself is: *Is this belief vibrationally compatible with my desire?* Because if it is not, then you cannot achieve your desire. So try to say or think something that feels better, that is more compatible with your desire. If you continue to try, you will find something that feels better. And as you practice feeling better and continue to reach for better-feeling thoughts, you will train your vibration (and your point of attraction) to a place where only good things will come to you.

Some of your beliefs are of benefit to you, and some of them are not. Your awareness of the vibrational relativity between your active desire and your active beliefs will help you sort that out. You will discover that it is not difficult to find and activate beliefs that harmonize with your desires, and when you do, your intended desires will become your manifested reality.

ᬏᬏᬏ ᬏᬏᬏ

Chapter 14

Vibrational Relativity Regarding My Home

The following are some examples of the vibrational relativity between the common desires and the beliefs that we see in many people regarding their homes. First we will state a common desire that many people hold regarding their homes, and then we will list a series of common beliefs about that desire. And next, in brackets, following those beliefs, we will indicate the degree of vibrational compatibility.

For any desire to be realized by you, or before anything can manifest in your life experience, there must be vibrational compatibility between your desires and your beliefs.

As you read down each of the following lists, notice the feeling of the lessening of resistance—or the improvement in the vibrational relationship—between the stated *desire* and the commonly associated *belief.*

Desire: *I want to be able to afford a fabulous home.*

Belief: I can't afford the kind of home I want to live in.
[This belief is vibrationally incompatible with the stated desire.]

Belief: There's some variance even in homes in a similar price range. [This belief is vibrationally more compatible with the stated desire.]

Belief: It's possible, under the right circumstances, to find hidden treasures out there in the housing market. [This belief is even more vibrationally compatible with the stated desire.]

Desire: *I want to be able to control my personal environment.*

Belief: Even though our neighborhood has regulations, they're not enforced. My neighbors do as they please, having no consideration for how that impacts me. [This belief is vibrationally incompatible with the stated desire.]

Belief: My neighbors, for the most part, want a comfortable neighborhood for themselves, also. [This belief is vibrationally more compatible with the stated desire.]

Belief: For the most part, things go quite well in my neighborhood. [This belief is even more vibrationally compatible with the stated desire.]

Desire: *I want my home to be safe.*

Belief: Anyone and everyone has access to this neighborhood, and there's no way of protecting my property. [This belief is vibrationally incompatible with the stated desire.]

Belief: When I think about all of the homes and all of the belongings that people have, I realize that it's really a rare thing when someone's property or things are violated. [This belief is vibrationally more compatible with the stated desire.]

Belief: My property isn't being singled out with negative intention. All is well with my home. [This belief is even more vibrationally compatible with the stated desire.]

Desire: *I want my home to contain modern conveniences for ease and comfort.*

Belief: There are many things that can be purchased that make life easier and more comfortable, but they cost a great deal of money. [This belief is vibrationally incompatible with the stated desire.]

Belief: Tools and appliances that bring the most ease are readily available and affordable to me. [This belief is vibrationally more compatible with the stated desire.]

Belief: There are many things that I can do, which I have complete control over, which will add both ease and comfort to my home environment. [This belief is even more vibrationally compatible with the stated desire.]

Desire: *I want to own my home.*

Belief: To own my own home I need a large down payment, and I'm already spending everything I'm making. [This belief is vibrationally incompatible with the stated desire.]

Belief: At this time, the economy is such that nearly anyone (if they really want to) can own their own home. [This belief is vibrationally more compatible with the stated desire.]

Belief: I know that when I finally decide I want to purchase a home, I'll be able to figure out how to do it. [This belief is even more vibrationally compatible with the stated desire.]

Desire: *I want to find a home that will satisfy me for all of the days of my life.*

Belief: Even if that perfect place is out there somewhere, I don't know how I'll find it, if it will be available, or how I could afford it. [This belief is vibrationally incompatible with the stated desire.]

Belief: Experience has shown me that I'm a changing Being, and my tastes and desires relative to all things are changing. [This belief is vibrationally more compatible with the stated desire.]

Belief: It's not necessary for me to find a home that will please me forever. I'll find one that pleases me for now, and then I'll make another decision later. [This belief is even more vibrationally compatible with the stated desire.]

Some people argue that simply reaching for things that feel a little better seems of little consequence to changing anything. "What good does it do to just say different words? Isn't that just a form of denial? I've been taught that I should tell it like it is, and that I should face up to reality."

We want you to understand that this process will help you create a different and more pleasing reality. If you continue to see things as they are and talk about them as they are, nothing can change. You cannot instantly see them in a very different way than they are, but you can easily mold your perspective into increasingly better-feeling places on every subject of importance to you. And as you make those vibrational shifts and *feel* the emotional improvements, the vibrational discrepancy between your desires and beliefs will be resolved; you will come into perfect alignment with what you desire, and what manifests in your life experience will absolutely reflect those changes.

Why would you want to accept or "face a reality" that is __not__ pleasing when you can create a reality that __is__ pleasing?

Chapter 15

Vibrational Relativity Regarding My Work

The following are some examples of the vibrational relativity between the common desires and the beliefs that we see in many people regarding their work, employment, or occupation. First we will state a common desire that many people hold regarding their work, and then we will list a series of common beliefs about that desire. And next, in brackets, following those beliefs, we will indicate the degree of vibrational compatibility.

For any desire to be realized by you, or before anything can manifest in your life experience, there must be vibrational compatibility between your desires and your beliefs.

As you read down each of the following lists, notice the feeling of the lessening of resistance—or the improvement in the vibrational relationship—between the stated *desire* and the commonly associated *belief.*

Desire: *I want work that is more satisfying.*

Belief: This is what I've been trained to do, but I'm tired of doing it. [This belief is vibrationally incompatible with the stated desire.]

> *Belief:* My work *was* more interesting in the beginning when it was new to me. [This belief is vibrationally more compatible with the stated desire.]

Belief: In the same way I learned to do this work, there are many other new things that I could learn to do. [This belief is even more vibrationally compatible with the stated desire.]

Desire: *I want work that brings me more monetary compensation.*

Belief: It isn't possible to make more money doing this, because this is what people who do what I do, make. [This belief is vibrationally incompatible with the stated desire.]

Belief: There are companies who pay better than others, and there are many other companies than the one I am currently involved with. [This belief is vibrationally more compatible with the stated desire.]

Belief: It's possible to find a company that sees greater value in what I have to offer. [This belief is even more vibrationally compatible with the stated desire.]

Desire: *I want a work environment that is more pleasing.*

Belief: This work environment is a disgusting place. [This belief is vibrationally incompatible with the stated desire.]

Belief: By implementing some good ideas, and with a little ingenuity, I can improve my immediate surroundings. Who knows, I may start a trend. [This belief is vibrationally more compatible with the stated desire.]

Belief: By visualizing the implementation of a few good ideas, and with my determination to see it all *differently,* this place doesn't feel so bad after all. [This belief is even more vibrationally compatible with the stated desire.]

Desire: *I want to work with people who are nice to be around.*

Belief: I have no personal control over the people who are hired to work here, and the person I share my office with is very annoying. [This belief is vibrationally incompatible with the stated desire.]

> *Belief:* I see a variety of personalities in my workplace. [This belief is vibrationally more compatible with the stated desire.]

> > *Belief:* I really like that friendly girl who answers the telephone. [This belief is even more vibrationally compatible with the stated desire.]

Desire: *I want to do work that stimulates my personal growth.*

Belief: I feel stuck in a job that has no opportunities to expand. [This belief is vibrationally incompatible with the stated desire.]

> *Belief:* There are probably opportunities for expansion around me that I've been overlooking. [This belief is vibrationally more compatible with the stated desire.]

> > *Belief:* The work I want must be out there, and I'll know it when I see it. [This belief is even more vibrationally compatible with the stated desire.]

Desire: *I want to be free.*

Belief: I have no freedom at work, and it seems like I'm always there. [This belief is vibrationally incompatible with the stated desire.]

Belief: My work does have variety, and some of it is pleasurable to experience. [This belief is vibrationally more compatible with the stated desire.]

Belief: It's my choice to be here, and I could choose to leave if I wanted to. [This belief is even more vibrationally compatible with the stated desire.]

When you are interacting with other people, it sometimes feels a bit more challenging to you to choose your own thoughts. It seems so natural to observe the conditions that are surrounding you and then to have a knee-jerk reaction to whatever those conditions are. But when you discover your ability to sift through those experiences and deliberately choose better-feeling perspectives, you will begin to understand your creative invincibility. In time, you will be able to maintain your connection to your own desires no matter what is going on around you. And as you learn to exercise your vibrational control, only good-feeling situations will find their way to you.

ఆఫ్ ఆఫ్ ఆఫ్ ఔు ఔు ఔు

Chapter 16

Vibrational Relativity Regarding My Relationships

The following are some examples of the vibrational relativity between the common desires and the beliefs that we see in many people regarding their relationships. First we will state a common desire that many people hold regarding their relationships, and then we will list a series of common beliefs about that desire. And next, in brackets, following those beliefs, we will indicate the degree of vibrational compatibility.

For any desire to be realized by you, or before anything can manifest in your life experience, there must be vibrational compatibility between your desires and your beliefs.

As you read down each of the following lists, notice the feeling of the lessening of resistance—or the improvement in the vibrational relationship—between the stated *desire* and the commonly associated *belief.*

Desire: *I want to find my perfect partner.*

Belief: I've been looking for so long. All of the really great people have already found their mates. [This belief is vibrationally incompatible with the stated desire.]

> *Belief:* I've only recently decided that I'm really ready for a mate. I'm glad my mate didn't get here before I was

ready. [This belief is vibrationally more compatible with the stated desire.]

Belief: When I make up my mind about something, it usually works out for me. [This belief is even more vibrationally compatible with the stated desire.]

Desire: *I want to improve my relationship with my mate.*

Belief: Everything I do seems to make my mate angry. [This belief is vibrationally incompatible with the stated desire.]

Belief: We had a great relationship when we first came together. [This belief is vibrationally more compatible with the stated desire.]

Belief: I'd love to return to those old feelings of really loving each other. [This belief is even more vibrationally compatible with the stated desire.]

Desire: *I want a better relationship with my parent(s).*

Belief: Even though I've been an adult for years, my mother still thinks she needs to tell me what to do. [This belief is vibrationally incompatible with the stated desire.]

Belief: My father's interest in me comes from a place of wanting me to have a good life. [This belief is vibrationally more compatible with the stated desire.]

Belief: My mother really does mean well, and what she says and does actually has little or no effect on my life. [This belief is even more vibrationally compatible with the stated desire.]

Desire: *I want a better relationship with my child(ren).*

Belief: My child seems to think that I'm the path through which everything she wants will come to her. [This belief is vibrationally incompatible with the stated desire.]

> *Belief:* When I was his age, I looked at life very differently than I do now—but not so different from the way he sees it, I suppose. [This belief is vibrationally more compatible with the stated desire.]

>> *Belief:* We're both continually changing, and that is such a good thing. [This belief is even more vibrationally compatible with the stated desire.]

Desire: *I want a better relationship with my employer.*

Belief: My employer doesn't seem to be aware of how much value I am to him. [This belief is vibrationally incompatible with the stated desire.]

> *Belief:* I want to make a noticeable difference at work. [This belief is vibrationally more compatible with the stated desire.]

>> *Belief:* I feel good about the work I do regardless of anyone else's awareness of it. [This belief is even more vibrationally compatible with the stated desire.]

Desire: *I want to get along better with people.*

Belief: People don't seem to understand me. I'm like a fish out of water. [This belief is vibrationally incompatible with the stated desire.]

Belief: There is great variety in people. I do resonate well with some of them. [This belief is vibrationally more compatible with the stated desire.]

Belief: I do have a good relationship with that person. [This belief is even more vibrationally compatible with the stated desire.]

As you are beginning to deliberately train your perspective toward those better-feeling beliefs, *we always encourage you to start with something easy.* In other words, do not focus upon your most challenging relationship and use it as your test case to see how good you are at improving your vibrational relativity between where you are and where you want to be. Once you have shown yourself that you can easily, on most subjects, find improved perspectives, *then* you can focus upon those more challenging situations. In time, you will know that you have absolute control over the way you feel, over your point of focus, over your point of attraction, and over everything that comes into your own life experience.

≥§≥§≥§ ξ≈ξ≈ξ≈

Chapter 17

Vibrational Relativity
Regarding My Financial Abundance

The following are some examples of the vibrational relativity between the common desires and the beliefs that we see in many people regarding their financial abundance. First we will state a common desire that many people hold regarding money or about abundance, and then we will list a series of common beliefs about that desire. And next, in brackets, following those beliefs, we will indicate the degree of vibrational compatibility.

For any desire to be realized by you, or before anything can manifest in your life experience, there must be vibrational compatibility between your desires and your beliefs.

As you read down each of the following lists, notice the feeling of the lessening of resistance—or the improvement in the vibrational relationship—between the stated *desire* and the commonly associated *belief.*

Desire: *I want more money.*

Belief: I'm so tired of not being able to afford to do the things I want to do. [This belief is vibrationally incompatible with the stated desire.]

Belief: If I plan well, I can shift things around so that my money goes further. [This belief is vibrationally more compatible with the stated desire.]

Belief: I'm so glad I have enough money to put toward this thing that I want. [This belief is even more vibrationally compatible with the stated desire.]

Desire: *I want money to come to me more easily.*

Belief: It seems like too much of my life is spent earning money. [This belief is vibrationally incompatible with the stated desire.]

Belief: Surely there are things to do that earn more money per hour. [This belief is vibrationally more compatible with the stated desire.]

Belief: I'm glad I have this marketable skill that pays the bills. [This belief is even more vibrationally compatible with the stated desire.]

Desire: *I want to feel good about having money.*

Belief: My mother said that money doesn't make you happy. In fact, she believes that it ruins lives. [This belief is vibrationally incompatible with the stated desire.]

Belief: I've seen people with and without money who were happy, and I've seen people with and without money who were sad. Money doesn't have to ruin your life. [This belief is vibrationally more compatible with the stated desire.]

Belief: Money feels freeing to me. It lifts limitations, and it affords opportunities. [This belief is even more vibrationally compatible with the stated desire.]

Desire: *I want to be comfortable about others not having money.*

Belief: I love my luxurious new car, but I feel bad that that man has no place to live. [This belief is vibrationally incompatible with the stated desire.]

> *Belief:* I understand that my not buying that car would not then mean that that man would have a place to live. [This belief is vibrationally more compatible with the stated desire.]

> > *Belief:* Everyone has exactly as much money as they expect and allow themselves to have. [This belief is even more vibrationally compatible with the stated desire.]

Desire: *I want to come into financial balance.*

Belief: No matter how hard I try or how much I work, something always seems to come up that keeps me from getting ahead. [This belief is vibrationally incompatible with the stated desire.]

> *Belief:* I don't have much control over how much money will come in this week, but I do have some control over how much I spend. [This belief is vibrationally more compatible with the stated desire.]

> > *Belief:* I'm gradually coming into balance. [This belief is even more vibrationally compatible with the stated desire.]

Desire: *I want to be free of debt.*

Belief: I'm so tired of being in so much debt. My monthly payments take such a big piece of my paycheck that there's hardly anything left with which to enjoy life. [This belief is vibrationally incompatible with the stated desire.]

> *Belief:* Responsible debt is not such a bad thing; it has allowed me to enjoy some things sooner than I would have been able to otherwise. [This belief is vibrationally more compatible with the stated desire.]

>> *Belief:* With or without debt I can achieve financial balance. Some of the most successful entities on the planet have some of the largest debts. [This belief is even more vibrationally compatible with the stated desire.]

When you decide that you are going to improve the vibrational relationship between what you __want__ regarding money and what you currently __believe__ regarding money, you will begin to see immediate results. Because dollars affect your life in so many different ways, you think about them more often. So, if you are making some effort to feel better whenever the subject of money comes up, you will quickly shift your point of attraction. The improvement in the vibrational relationship between your *desires* and your *beliefs* will be apparent right away.

ᴏᴈ ᴏᴈ ᴏᴈ ᵷᴐ ᵷᴐ ᵷᴐ

Chapter 18

Vibrational Relativity Regarding My World

The following are some examples of the vibrational relativity between the common desires and the beliefs that we see in many people regarding their world. First we will state a common desire that many people hold regarding the world, and then we will list a series of common beliefs about that desire. And next, in brackets, following those beliefs, we will indicate the degree of vibrational compatibility.

For any desire to be realized by you, or before anything can manifest in your life experience, there must be vibrational compatibility between your desires and your beliefs.

As you read down each of the following lists, notice the feeling of the lessening of resistance—or the improvement in the vibrational relationship—between the stated *desire* and the commonly associated *belief.*

Desire: *I want the world to be a happier place.*

Belief: There's so much suffering in the world. [This belief is vibrationally incompatible with the stated desire.]

Belief: I've lived quite a good life. [This belief is vibrationally more compatible with the stated desire.]

Belief: Look how happy *that* little girl is. [This belief is even more vibrationally compatible with the stated desire.]

Desire: *I want the people of the world to get along with one another.*

Belief: It seems as if there are so many conflicts and wars happening today. [This belief is vibrationally incompatible with the stated desire.]

Belief: Not *all* people are involved in conflicts. [This belief is vibrationally more compatible with the stated desire.]

Belief: There are many people around the world who are living in joy. [This belief is even more vibrationally compatible with the stated desire.]

Desire: *I want the world to be a safe place.*

Belief: What if something catastrophic like an earthquake, tidal wave, or nuclear explosion disrupts the Well-Being of our planet? [This belief is vibrationally incompatible with the stated desire.]

Belief: We've long lived with the threats of those occurrences—as well as the reality of them—and we continue not only to exist but to thrive. [This belief is vibrationally more compatible with the stated desire.]

Belief: The Well-Being of this planet certainly does appear to be dominant. [This belief is even more vibrationally compatible with the stated desire.]

Desire: *I want the world to be a healthy place.*

Belief: There are so many things in the world today that threaten our health. [This belief is vibrationally incompatible with the stated desire.]

  Belief: While some places seem truly toxic, there are many that are really thriving. [This belief is vibrationally more compatible with the stated desire.]

    Belief: Our planet has tremendous regenerating capabilities. [This belief is even more vibrationally compatible with the stated desire.]

Desire: *I want to experience more of this world.*

Belief: This world is so vast, and I'm experiencing such a small part of it. I feel like I'm missing out on so much. [This belief is vibrationally incompatible with the stated desire.]

  Belief: Technology makes the world so much more accessible. I can see places and gather information about them before I visit them personally. [This belief is vibrationally more compatible with the stated desire.]

    Belief: I love exploring my world. I'm going to start paying more attention *wherever* I am. [This belief is even more vibrationally compatible with the stated desire.]

In earlier times, before the technology of your planet gave you the ability to see what is happening in every village or city on your planet, it was possible to observe those around you and, for the most part, maintain your awareness of Well-Being. But in these modern times, with so much emphasis placed on pockets of unrest, war, and natural calamities, your observation of your world—through the negatively slanted view of your news media—

gives you an enormously distorted perspective of the Well-Being of your planet.

Nothing fosters your perception of your lack of empowerment more than constant graphic reminders of tragedies occurring that you have no personal involvement in, or the power to change.

It is our desire that you come to understand that those things are not your work. *Your work is to tend to your own Energy Balance, and when you do, your world will come into perfect alignment.*

ᵹᵹᵹ ᶝᶝᶝ

Chapter 19

Vibrational Relativity Regarding My Government

The following are some examples of the vibrational relativity between the common desires and the beliefs that we see in many people regarding their government. First we will state a common desire that many people hold regarding their government, and then we will list a series of common beliefs about that desire. And next, in brackets, following those beliefs, we will indicate the degree of vibrational compatibility.

For any desire to be realized by you, or before anything can manifest in your life experience, there must be vibrational compatibility between your desires and your beliefs.

As you read down each of the following lists, notice the feeling of the lessening of resistance—or the improvement in the vibrational relationship—between the stated *desire* and the commonly associated *belief.*

Desire: *I want wise and responsible leaders at the head of my government.*

Belief: The leaders of my government seem foolish and irresponsible. [This belief is vibrationally incompatible with the stated desire.]

Belief: There probably are some talented and wise people, with a strong background and understanding in various areas, working in our government. [This belief is vibrationally more compatible with the stated desire.]

> *Belief:* I liked what I heard from that government official regarding this issue. [This belief is even more vibrationally compatible with the stated desire.]

Desire: *I want my government to reflect the desires and interests of the people it represents.*

Belief: Politicians tell us one thing while they're trying to get elected, but then once they're in office, they do what best serves their own selfish interests. [This belief is vibrationally incompatible with the stated desire.]

> *Belief:* Our government is an extremely complex entity. While some aspects of it seem out of balance, there are obvious aspects of government that effectively serve the public. [This belief is vibrationally more compatible with the stated desire.]

> > *Belief:* There are so many advantages to living here in this wonderful nation. [This belief is even more vibrationally compatible with the stated desire.]

Desire: *I want my government to understand that it exists to serve the people it represents.*

Belief: Our government has become a self-perpetuating agency that seems to have forgotten that it exists to serve the people who've elected it. [This belief is vibrationally incompatible with the stated desire.]

Belief: While our government is often inefficient, I don't believe that we would be better off without it. [This belief is vibrationally more compatible with the stated desire.]

Belief: Our government is comprised of many departments and many individuals with good intentions. [This belief is even more vibrationally compatible with the stated desire.]

Desire: *I want my government to be fair and balanced.*

Belief: The administration of our current government isn't even trying to acknowledge that there may be other points of view that have merit. [This belief is vibrationally incompatible with the stated desire.]

Belief: I recognize that my government seems most unfair and imbalanced when their views disagree with my own. Maybe our disagreement is part of the balancing process. [This belief is vibrationally more compatible with the stated desire.]

Belief: Even though, at times, I disagree with the direction of those in office, our system of government assures that no administration can remain in office indefinitely. And so, the balance eventually comes, even though it may take some time. [This belief is even more vibrationally compatible with the stated desire.]

Desire: *I want a government that is well respected by other governments and by the people of the world.*

Belief: I'm embarrassed by the actions of my government, which seem arrogant and self-serving to many other nations. [This belief is vibrationally incompatible with the stated desire.]

> *Belief:* My opinion about my government, and the response of the people of other nations, is based on very limited information. [This belief is vibrationally more compatible with the stated desire.]

>> *Belief:* The presence of my nation and the efforts of my government, past and present, have added tremendous value to this world. [This belief is even more vibrationally compatible with the stated desire.]

Desire: *I want a government that is fiscally responsible.*

Belief: If my government were a normal business, continuing to spend more than it earns, it would have been bankrupt and out of business years ago. [This belief is vibrationally incompatible with the stated desire.]

> *Belief:* I realize that my concern around my government's fiscal irresponsibility is based more upon my fear of what the future will bring than about what's actually happening right now. [This belief is vibrationally more compatible with the stated desire.]

>> *Belief:* Even though the size of our government is increasing, and the money it is spending is ever greater, the overall life experience of the people of this nation has been steadily rising. [This belief is even more vibrationally compatible with the stated desire.]

Many people, in the beginning of their decision to tend to the balance of their own Energies, balk at the idea of giving someone with whom they vehemently disagree the benefit of the doubt. *There is no point of view, regarding governmental issues (or any issues, for that matter) that we desire to guide you toward or away from. It is only our desire that you find a way to come into alignment with you. For when you do, your own life and world will reflect that balance, and until you do, there is not enough action in the world that can compensate for the misalignment of Energies.*

ᘓ ᘓ ᘓ ᘔ ᘔ ᘔ

Chapter 20

Realigning with Your Vibration of Well-Being

If you are like most people, reading through the previous examples of *desires* and *beliefs* has caused an activation of many vibrations within you. You have probably felt your own personal agreement, or disagreement, with some of what you have just read, for it is easy to lose sight of your true objective when you read through a list of subjects that may touch upon some of the specifics of your own life. But we want you to remember the important premise that we are putting forth here: *It is necessary for the vibration of your desire and the vibration of your belief to match, for without that vibrational alignment, you are not in alignment. And as long as you are out of alignment, you cannot allow the Well-Being that you have been asking for to flow into your experience.*

As you read through the previous examples (and at the end of this chapter we encourage you to go back and read through them again), you may have recognized that you agreed with the *desires* (or some of them) that we offered as examples, and that you *also* agreed with many of the first examples we offered of a *belief* that was incompatible with the stated *desire*.

In other words, it is very common for a person to: *desire more money and believe that there simply is not enough money.*

It is very common for a person to: *desire to lose unwanted body weight and believe that no diets work for them.*

It is very common for a person to: _desire_ _a healthy body and_ _believe_ _that there is no cure for this physical condition._

Balancing Vibrations Between Your Desires and Beliefs

The purpose of the examples we have offered has been to help you understand that it is your work to bring vibrational balance between your _desires_ and your _beliefs_. If your body is, in this moment, healthy; or if right now you have all the money you can possibly spend, you could look at your current state of affairs and speak about them—as they are—without causing a vibrational mismatch between your _desires_ and your _beliefs_. But if, on any subject, things are _not_ the way you want them to be, you cannot continue to speak about them as they _are_ without causing vibrational discord between your _desire_ and your _belief_. And that vibrational discord will prevent you from realizing your desire. And remember, your emotions will, in the moment, indicate that vibrational imbalance.

This Is Your Ultimate Balancing of Energy

As you read back through the examples of beliefs and desires that we have offered here, try to be aware of your feeling of discord between the stated desire and the first example of belief that we offered. And then notice if you feel relief as you read the second example of belief, and then even more relief as you read the third example.

To begin experiencing wonderful improvement in your own life experience—on any subject that is important to you—you have only to understand and then deliberately improve upon the vibrational relationship between your _desire_ and your _belief_—this is the ultimate balancing of Energy.

It is easy to get lost in the discussion of right or wrong, or whether something is true or not. Many will argue, "But this _is_ what is happening, and I cannot deny that this _is_ what is happening." They will argue that there are many others who agree with them about this injustice or that inappropriate situation. But we want you to realize that your attention to those things—which activate within you opposing vibrations to your own desires—will prevent you from ever finding the improvement you are seeking. You cannot continue to encourage a vibrational activation within yourself that opposes your own intentions and ever hope to realize those intentions. You must first bring the vibration of your Being into alignment.

◆◆◆ ◆◆◆

Chapter 21

Finding Vibrational Alignment with Your Inner Being

[handwritten annotation: Inner Being Knows what you want need alignment c̄ Inner Being to manifest Inner Being Innerfrey / no want]

It is of great value to have continual awareness of the vibrational relativity between *your* current point of focus and the point of focus of your *Inner Being. If you will remember that the attention of your Inner Being is upon the <u>outcome</u> that you desire—and then if you will try to find vibrational alignment with your Inner Being—you will then find vibrational alignment with your desired outcome.*

There are many valuable and good-feeling reasons to try to align with your Inner Being/Source/Who-You-Really-Are:

- That Non-Physical part of you is the sum of all that you have become and is therefore extremely wise.

- That Non-Physical part of you is Source Energy and is therefore the vibrational equivalent to love and Well-Being.

- That vibration of your Inner Being is Pure, Positive Energy (resistance free by your standards) and is therefore extremely powerful and effective.

So when you make the effort to come into closer vibrational alignment with that Non-Physical part of yourself, you open yourself to that wisdom, love, Well-Being, and power. When you are in alignment with your Source, you experience the clarity, vitality, enthusiasm, passion, and Well-Being that is natural to you.

Am I Allowing, or Resisting, My Well-Being?

We refer to your vibrational alignment with your Source as *allowing*. We refer to your vibrational misalignment with your Source as *less allowing*. The more out of alignment you become, and the less you allow your Connection to your Source, the more you become in a state of vibrational *resistance:* resistance to thriving, resistance to wellness, resistance to clarity, resistance to abundance, and resistance to your personal Well-Being. *Sensitivity to your emotions will help you to be aware of just how much allowing or resisting you are doing in any moment in time: <u>The better you feel, the more you are allowing your Connection to your Source. The worse you feel, the less you are allowing your Connection to your Source.</u>*

Your Most Important Decision to Make

When you decide to make your awareness of the vibrational relativity between you and your Source of extreme importance, you will have made the most important decision that you could ever make, for you have now consciously activated your own personal Guidance System, and you will never be lost again. When you understand your emotions and what they mean, and so, are able to deliberately improve the way you feel through a deliberate choosing of increasingly better-feeling thoughts—there will be no intent that you cannot easily accomplish. . . . All things that you desire will flow quickly and easily into your experience.

Now, as new intentions continue to be born within you, your belief in your ability to accomplish *them* will grow as well. You will begin to feel free, invincible, eager, and joyful. You will feel as your Inner Being feels—enjoying the contrast that produces the desire that summons the Energy that creates worlds, riding the wave of this fast-moving current out here on this Leading Edge of creation.

In simple terms, the vibrational relationship between you and your Inner Being translates into the difference between emotions that feel good and emotions that feel bad. Emotions that feel good indicate alignment with, or allowing of, your Source; while emotions that feel bad indicate misalignment with, or resistance to, the Energy of your Source.

Freedom, or Lack of Such, As Perceptual

When you consider the extent of emotions that range from the good-feeling ones such as joy, love, and appreciation . . . all the way down to depression, despair, fear, and grief, can you feel how *empowering* those good-feeling emotions are, and how *disempowering* those bad-feeling emotions are? Can you not sense the feeling of freedom on one end of the scale, and the lack of freedom on the other?

The good-feeling end of the *Emotional Guidance Scale* matches the vibration of *perceived* freedom. The bad-feeling end of the *Emotional Guidance Scale* matches the vibration of *perceived* lack of freedom. Freedom or lack of freedom is truly perceptual because—whether you understand it or not—you are absolutely free, for no one can get inside of you and offer your vibration for you, for it is only your own vibrational offering that affects your personal life experience. And so it is of tremendous value for you to acknowledge, from your own point of view, the feeling of absolute freedom or empowerment that some emotions signal and the feelings of utter bondage or disempowerment that are pointed out by others.

Your Inner Being, or Source, understands that you are free, under all conditions, to create what you desire, but when you *perceive* that you are *not* free, those negative emotions, which ensue from depression, despair, or fear, point out your misalignment. Your Inner Being, or Source, understands that you are free, under all conditions, to create what you desire; so when you *perceive* that you *are* free, you feel those confirming, matching, aligning feelings of positive emotion that indicate your alignment with your Source.

Now, when you conclude that nothing is more important than that you feel good, you have come to the most important realization of all, for you have now decided to deliberately *manage the vibrational relationship between you and your Source. You have decided to use the Guidance System that you were born with to monitor and control the vibrational relativity between your current focus, and subsequent vibration, and that of your Inner Being. You have decided to tend to your Connection with your Source. You have decided to thrive rather than pinch off your Connection. You have chosen clarity, vitality, eagerness, abundance of all things you consider to be good—and joy.*

Chapter 22

Your Point of Attraction and the Relief Factor

We are going to offer a very wise, but also very obvious, statement here: *You are where you are.* *What you have been thinking and what you currently are thinking has resulted in your creation, in your life experience, of who-is. And so, that's that! However, we want you to turn your full attention to the vibrational relativity between where you are right now, and where you want to be—for that is where all of your power is. That is where the thrill of creative genius lies.*

That vibrational variance between where you are and where you want to be is the creative arena that you have come forth to play within: the Leading Edge of creation. This is what you have come forth to experience and enjoy—and to never complete.

So where you stand and how you feel right now equals your vibrational point of attraction. And if you are aware, you can tell by the way you *feel* how your perception of where you are, right now, matches, or does not match, the vibration of your Source.

If, right now, you are intent upon achieving the best match that you can with the vibration of your Source, then you will be reaching for, or feeling for, better and better-feeling thoughts— *and as you find a better-feeling thought, a feeling of relief will be your experience.*

The _Emotional Guidance Scale,_
from Allowing to Resistance

Imagine an _Emotional Guidance Scale_ with the good-feeling thoughts on one end and the bad-feeling thoughts on the other. And now, acknowledge that the end that feels good equals _allowing,_ and the end that feels bad equals _resistance._ So it is obvious that, depending upon your choice of thoughts, you could move toward either end of this scale. It is also obvious that the further you are from one end of the scale, the closer you are to the other end. In other words, this thought feels better; _this_ thought feels worse. This better-feeling thought indicates allowing; _this_ worse-feeling thought indicates resistance. . . .

A Scale of Your Emotions
Would Look Like This:

1. Joy/Knowledge/Empowerment/Freedom/Love/ Appreciation
2. Passion
3. Enthusiasm/Eagerness/Happiness
4. Positive Expectation/Belief
5. Optimism
6. Hopefulness
7. Contentment
8. Boredom
9. Pessimism
10. Frustration/Irritation/Impatience
11. "Overwhelment"
12. Disappointment
13. Doubt
14. Worry
15. Blame
16. Discouragement

17. Anger
18. Revenge
19. Hatred/Rage
20. Jealousy
21. Insecurity/Guilt/Unworthiness
22. Fear/Grief/Depression/Despair/Powerlessness

disconnected from God, Spirit, Source — out of the vortex

Since the same words are often used to mean different things, and different words are often used to mean the same things, these word labels for your emotions are not absolutely accurate for every person who feels the emotion. In fact, giving word labels to the emotions could cause confusion and distract you from the real purpose of your *Emotional Guidance Scale.*

The thing that matters most is that you consciously reach for a feeling that is improved. The word for the feeling is not important.

Continually Reach for Relief from Resistance

A rather effective way of balancing your Energy is to continually reach for feelings of relief. A feeling of *relief* always indicates an improvement in your vibration, and it always means a releasing of *resistance,* or an increasing of *allowing—and if we were standing in your physical shoes, we would make the relief factor the most important part of our personal awareness.*

When you continually look for a way of looking at everything that feels slightly better than what you are currently feeling, you are getting closer and closer to seeing your world as your Inner Being sees it. And, in the process, you will be leaving resistance behind.

Your own resistance is the only factor that keeps you from realizing all of the wonderful things that you desire.

Illness is about resistance.

Confusion is about resistance.

Poverty is about resistance.

Sadness is about resistance.

Car accidents are about resistance. . . .

All things that you consider to be bad exist only because of resistance to your natural Well-Being.

There Is Not a Source of "Unwanted"

You do not walk into a room and look for the *dark switch,* for you understand that there is not a switch that floods darkness into the room, which covers the source of light. And, by the same principle, there is not a source of sickness, badness, or evil, but merely a practiced resistance to the natural Source of Well-Being.

Reaching for relief, moment by moment, thought by thought, and subject by subject, will bring you increasingly closer to your Source of Well-Being. When you care about how you feel, and you deliberately try to look at things in ways that feel better and better to you (making the *best* of things instead of the *worst* of things), you will allow more and resist less—and the circumstances and events of your life will begin to reflect those changes immediately. *Relief* indicates the releasing of resistance, which is the same thing as moving toward more *allowing.* It is an effective use of your *Emotional Guidance System.*

⊷ ⊷ ⊷ ⊶ ⊶ ⊶

Chapter 23

The Balancing of Energies for Joyful Creation

The variety, or contrast, that surrounds you is of tremendous value, for it is the data from which your personal preferences and desires are born. You are a creator, and you create through the power of your focus. In every moment that you live, and with every experience you live, the variety of your life inspires the launching of new desires and the amending of previous desires. And so, focused desire never ceases to flow forth from you.

The expansion of the Universe is dependent upon this process: Contrast causes a focusing of desire, and then, through the *Law of Attraction,* that desire is answered by Source Energy. In other words, when you ask, it is always given.

Many argue that they have been asking, but they are not getting what they have been asking for. And we explain that anytime anyone, from any perspective, asks for anything, it is always given. But the *asking* that we are referring to is not the formulating of words or sentences, but the emanation of vibrations that exude naturally from you as you explore the contrast. For you cannot cease asking; asking is the most natural and most important result of the contrasting environment in which you are focused.

The reason (the only reason) that people ever find themselves in a position where they have been asking for something that they are not receiving is because they are holding themselves vibrationally apart from their own desire—the vibrational frequencies of what they want, and what is dominantly active within them, must balance.

Examples of Balancing Contrasting Vibrational Frequencies

The following examples will illustrate how you can benefit from the natural contrast of your physical environment by utilizing your *Emotional Guidance System* and deliberately improving the vibrational relationship between your desires and beliefs. *These examples will demonstrate the process of the Deliberate Balancing of Energies for the purpose of joyful creation:*

Current Contrasting Situation: First, we will describe a common situation of *what-is.* (Notice the beliefs that are active within the current situation.)

Resulting Desire(s): Next we will list the desires that are born out of that contrast. (For whenever you are in a situation where you know what you *do not* want, in that moment of contrast you always know more clearly what it is that you *do* want.)

Resulting Emotion(s) or Indication(s) of Vibrational Discord: Then we will list the emotions that indicate the current active vibrations (beliefs).

Deliberate Effort to Improve the Vibrational Relationship Between My New Desire and My Current Belief: And now, we will offer a series of statements to assist in bringing the current active (belief) vibration into alignment with the desire. (As you read, see if you can feel the improvement in the vibrational relativity between the *desires* and the *beliefs.* Know that the feeling of relief indicates both the releasing of resistance and an improvement in the vibrational relationship between the *desire* and the *belief.* In other words, the better you feel, the more in balance your

Energies are. (Of course you could also say,
"The more in balance my Energies are—the
better I feel.")

Result: Finally, we will point out the specific improvement in the vibrational relationship between the *desire* and the *belief* as is
evidenced by the better-feeling emotion.

There is no understanding that will ever be of more importance
to you than this, for once you understand the process of deliberately
bringing the vibration of your *beliefs* into alignment with the
vibrations of your *intentions,* you will be the Deliberate Creator of
your experience—and there will be no intentions that you cannot
fulfill.

*Remember, if the life you are living has the resources to produce
within you any specific desire, then the resources also exist for your full
receiving, or manifestation, of that desire.*

ॐ ॐ ॐ ॐ ॐ ॐ

Chapter 24

My Body

Contrasting Weight Situation: I'm 50 pounds overweight. I've tried many different diets. They all work to some extent, for a while, and I lose some weight . . . but then I gain it all back, plus more. *My clothes don't fit well; I don't like the way I look, and I don't know what to do.*

Resulting Desires: I want to find a way to lose weight. I want to be able to maintain a comfortable body weight. I want to feel good and look good.

Resulting Emotions or Indications of Vibrational Discord: *I feel frustrated. I feel discouraged.* (There's a significant vibrational discord between my desire and my beliefs.)

Deliberate Effort to Improve the Vibrational Relationship Between My New Desire and My Current Belief:

- I've had the experience of losing weight.

- I'm aware of some things that have worked for me.

- When I put my mind to something, I usually get results.

- I have weighed more than I do right now.

- I do have some clothes that I feel I look pretty good in.

- I especially enjoy wearing my new gray outfit.

    Result: (Vibrational relativity has improved.)

Contrasting Health Situation: I've received a medical diagnosis that frightens me. I'm especially worried about it because my parents have both been afflicted by the same condition, and I've heard that several other members of my family have even died from this.

Resulting Desire: I want to be healthy.

Resulting Emotion or Indication of Vibrational Discord: *I feel fear.* (There's a significant vibrational discord between my desire and my beliefs.)

Deliberate Effort to Improve the Vibrational Relationship Between My New Desire and My Current Belief:

- A diagnosis is not a death sentence.

- People *have* recovered from this.

- There are many degrees of sickness with the same label.

- There are mild cases of this disease.

- I haven't been feeling bad.

- I actually have a hearty body.

- I've always been quick to bounce back from sickness.

    Result: (Vibrational relativity has improved.)

Contrasting Fatigue Situation: I have no energy. I feel tired all of the time. I can barely get through the day. I'm having a hard time keeping up with the things I need to do, and I'm not enjoying anything because I'm so tired. *I feel so overwhelmed.*

Resulting Desires: I want more energy. I want to feel good.

Resulting Emotion or Indication of Vibrational Discord: *I feel overwhelmed.* (There's a significant vibrational discord between my desire and my beliefs.)

Deliberate Effort to Improve the Vibrational Relationship Between My New Desire and My Current Belief:

- I always manage to accomplish what is really necessary.

- When I decide, I can do whatever needs to be done.

- I do notice that my energy fluctuates.

- There are times when I feel much better than others.

Result: (Vibrational relativity has improved.)

Contrasting Physical-Decline Situation: I worry that my body is deteriorating. I don't have the energy that I once had, and I can't do the things I used to enjoy doing. I have aches and pains, my knees hurt when I walk, and I don't dare try to run anymore. I'm scared that it's going to get worse and worse. *I feel worried.*

Resulting Desires: I want my body to feel good. I want my body to be healthy all the days of my life.

Resulting Emotion or Indication of Vibrational Discord: *I feel worried.* (There's a significant vibrational discord between my desire and my beliefs.)

Deliberate Effort to Improve the Vibrational Relationship Between My New Desire and My Current Belief:

- I've been quite healthy most of my life.

- Even when I was much younger, my body sometimes felt stiff.

- I remember having sore muscles even back when I was in high school.

Result: (Vibrational relativity has improved.)

ఇ§ఇ§ఇ§ ఇ&ఇ&ఇ&

Chapter 25

My Home

Contrasting Home-Space Situation: My home is a mess. It's so small, and it has such inadequate storage that I don't have anywhere to put anything. And even when I do try to clean it up to get more organized, I just make a bigger mess than before. *I feel frustration. I feel overwhelmed.*

Resulting Desires: I want my house to be organized. I want my house to look better. I want to be able to find things.

Resulting Emotions or Indications of Vibrational Discord: *I feel frustration. I feel overwhelmed.* (There's a significant vibrational discord between my desire and my beliefs.)

Deliberate Effort to Improve the Vibrational Relationship Between My New Desire and My Current Belief:

- I've been more organized before than I am right now.

- I've lived in smaller places than this.

- I have more things in this space with me than I really need.

- I could get rid of some things, which would make more space.

- I don't have to do it all at once.

   Result: (Vibrational relativity has improved.)

Contrasting Home-Deterioration Situation: I've lived in the same place for a long time, and I'm tired of it. It doesn't meet our needs at all anymore, but we can't really afford to move. I even find myself looking for excuses to not be at home because I don't feel good when I'm there. *I feel frustration. I feel irritation. I feel pessimism.*

   Resulting Desires: I want a bigger, better home. I want to enjoy being at home. I want more money so that I can buy a better home.

   Resulting Emotions or Indications of Vibrational Discord: *I feel frustration. I feel irritation. I feel pessimism.* (There's a significant vibrational discord between my desire and my beliefs.)

   Deliberate Effort to Improve the Vibrational Relationship Between My New Desire and My Current Belief:

- I've accumulated some possessions here that please me.

- When we first moved here, I felt happy about it.

- We are able to afford this house.

- Making some improvements might feel interesting.

- Those improvements would also add value to my home.

   Result: (Vibrational relativity has improved.)

Contrasting Neighbors' Situation: I used to like this neighborhood, but then some people moved in next door, and they're just awful neighbors. Their dog uses our yard for a bathroom, they have three or four junker cars parked in their driveway instead of on the street in front of the house, and I'm embarrassed to have people over to visit. *I feel blame. I feel discouraged. I feel anger.*

Resulting Desires: I want to live in a nice neighborhood. I want to have more considerate neighbors.

Resulting Emotions or Indications of Vibrational Discord: *I feel blame. I feel discouraged. I feel anger.* (There's a significant vibrational discord between my desire and my beliefs.)

Deliberate Effort to Improve the Vibrational Relationship Between My New Desire and My Current Belief:

- My guests haven't commented about my neighbors.

- The people who lived next door before were very neat.

- These neighbors may not stay there for very long.

- They do have a nice little girl.

- I do feel good when I'm in our secluded back yard.

  Result: (Vibrational relativity has improved.)

Contrasting Home-Maintenance Situation: Our house is costing us a fortune just to keep things working. It wasn't built very well to begin with, and now it's ten years old and things are constantly breaking down. Every time I turn around, something else needs to be repaired. *I feel frustrated. I feel overwhelmed. I feel disappointed. I feel discouraged.*

Resulting Desires: I want the things in my house to work the way they're supposed to. I want a new house.

Resulting Emotions or Indications of Vibrational Discord: *I feel frustrated. I feel overwhelmed. I feel disappointed. I feel discouraged.* (There's a significant vibrational discord between my desire and my beliefs.)

Deliberate Effort to Improve the Vibrational Relationship Between My New Desire and My Current Belief:

- I do like to stay on top of things.

- I do have high standards about the things in my home.

- It's logical that more conveniences mean more maintenance.

- I do appreciate the many conveniences of this home.

- My family has been very happy in this house.

  Result: (Vibrational relativity has improved.)

Chapter 26

My Relationships

Contrasting Adult-Child Situation: I have an adult daughter who's always mad at me. No matter how much time I spend with her, it's never enough. When I *am* with her, she spends most of our time complaining about how we don't spend enough time together! I'm so busy, and I don't have much time to spend with her, but it's really not fun to be with her because of the way she feels. *I feel guilty. I feel angry. I feel disappointed.*

> **Resulting Desires:** I want to enjoy being with my daughter. I want my daughter to feel good about me. I want my daughter to be happy.
>
> > **Resulting Emotions or Indications of Vibrational Discord:** *I feel guilty. I feel angry. I feel disappointed.* (There's a significant vibrational discord between my desire and my beliefs.)
> >
> > > **Deliberate Effort to Improve the Vibrational Relationship Between My New Desire and My Current Belief:**
> > >
> > > - Our relationship (maybe all relationships) will continually change.

- We have had our ups and our downs . . .

- . . . and our ups.

- She has such a wonderful personality.

- She has a really nice boyfriend.

- I'm happy she cares about spending time with me.

  Result: (Vibrational relativity has improved.)

Contrasting Loneliness Situation: I don't have many friends. Really, I don't even have one really close friend, and it's not much fun going through life alone. I've had friendships in the past, but nothing that really clicked. It seems like people are just looking for what they can get out of me, but then they don't really want to give anything back to me. *I feel discouraged. I feel lonely.*

Resulting Desires: I want a really good friend. I want friendships that are mutually beneficial.

Resulting Emotions or Indications of Vibrational Discord: *I feel discouraged. I feel lonely.* (There's a significant vibrational discord between my desire and my beliefs.)

Deliberate Effort to Improve the Vibrational Relationship Between My New Desire and My Current Belief:

- I've always been quite independent.

- I don't enjoy the feeling of *being* needed, or of being *in* need.

- I do enjoy stimulating conversations.

- I do like funny things, and it's always fun to laugh with others.

Result: (Vibrational relativity has improved.)

Contrasting Marital Situation: I still love my wife, but our relationship is nothing like it used to be. When we were first married, I couldn't wait to see her at the end of the day, and now, to be honest, I sort of dread going home. She complains a lot about so many different things, and I think she blames me for everything that isn't going the way she wants it to. I don't want to leave, but it's sure not fun staying, either. *I feel frustration. I feel blame. I feel irritation.*

Resulting Desires: I want to look forward to being at home. I want to enjoy being with my wife. I want to be in love again. I want my wife to love me. I want my wife to be happy.

Resulting Emotions or Indications of Vibrational Discord: *I feel frustration. I feel blame. I feel irritation.* (There's a significant vibrational discord between my desire and my beliefs.)

Deliberate Effort to Improve the Vibrational Relationship Between My New Desire and My Current Belief:

- I remember meeting my wife for the first time.

- My wife has always worked hard at being efficient.

- An organized household is very important to my wife.

- My wife has created an efficient and organized home for us.

- My wife works out of the home, and yet she still maintains our house.

- My wife is a rather amazing person.

    Result: (Vibrational relativity has improved.)

Contrasting Meddling-Parent Situation: I haven't lived at home for over ten years, but my mother still thinks that she needs to tell me what to do, so I avoid her because I don't like being bossed around. And then she gets mad, and that's even worse. But when we're together, she treats me like I don't know how to live my own life. *I feel blame. I feel anger.*

Resulting Desires: I want my mother to back off and let me live my own life. I want my mother to be easier to be around. I want my mother to understand that I'm on my own and that I can make my own decisions.

Resulting Emotions or Indications of Vibrational Discord: *I feel blame. I feel anger.* (There's a significant vibrational discord between my desire and my beliefs.)

Deliberate Effort to Improve the Vibrational Relationship Between My New Desire and My Current Belief:

- Parents are praised for guiding their children.

- It must be hard to get used to doing something and then stop.

- I know that my mother wants me to have a good life.

- I can take her suggestions or leave them.

- Sometimes her suggestions are helpful.
- My mother's suggestions are certainly well intentioned.

Result: (Vibrational relativity has improved.)

৩৩৩ ৫৩৩

Chapter 27

My Work

Contrasting Co-worker Situation: I share an office with someone whom I can hardly stand to be around. She doesn't have a nice thing to say about much of anything, and she wants to talk all the time. She doesn't enjoy her job, and she treats me like I'm foolish when I want to do mine. I wish she'd either quit or get fired. Life is too short to have to spend so much time with someone so unpleasant. *I feel irritation. I feel blame. I feel anger.*

Resulting Desires: I want to work with people who are nice to be around. I want to feel good when I'm at work.

Resulting Emotions or Indications of Vibrational Discord: *I feel irritation. I feel blame. I feel anger.* (There's a significant vibrational discord between my desire and my beliefs.)

Deliberate Effort to Improve the Vibrational Relationship Between My New Desire and My Current Belief:

- I've learned to really focus when I'm at work.

- Because I'm really focusing, I'm getting a lot of work done.

- I don't know what is really bothering her.

- She does have a nice smile.

- I'm sure that she'd like to feel better at work, too.

  Result: (Vibrational relativity has improved.)

Contrasting Job Situation: I get paid pretty well, compared to a lot of other jobs around, but I don't look forward to going to work. I've been doing pretty much the same thing for a long time, and I don't feel stimulated at all. No one seems to notice what I do unless I make a mistake. The day goes by so slowly . . . and then I have to turn around and do it all again the next day. *I feel boredom. I feel pessimism.*

Resulting Desires: I want more exciting, stimulating work. I want to look forward to going to work. I want to feel eager about my job.

Resulting Emotions or Indications of Vibrational Discord: *I feel boredom. I feel pessimism.* (There's a significant vibrational discord between my desire and my beliefs.)

Deliberate Effort to Improve the Vibrational Relationship Between My New Desire and My Current Belief:

- When I dig into a task, I can enjoy it.

- Some things I enjoy more than others.

- Sometimes I make fun games out of tasks.

- I enjoy improving my method of accomplishing tasks.

- I think I'll try that regarding more of my tasks.

- I'm going to watch for more ways I can be of value.

- I really like to feel like I'm of value.

  Result: (Vibrational relativity has improved.)

Contrasting Acting-Career Situation: I've wanted to be an actress ever since I was a little girl. I took some classes and found out that I'm pretty good at it. I get some acting work from time to time, but nothing exciting, and nothing that I really want. It's hard. There are so many people applying for the same work that I am that it seems hopeless. Maybe I should just forget about it and go get a real job. *I feel disappointed. I feel discouraged.*

Resulting Desires: I want to get some great acting jobs. I want a job where I'll be recognized as a good actress. I want to get some jobs that will lead to more jobs.

Resulting Emotions or Indications of Vibrational Discord: *I feel disappointed. I feel discouraged.* (There's a significant vibrational discord between my desire and my beliefs.)

Deliberate Effort to Improve the Vibrational Relationship Between My New Desire and My Current Belief:

- I'm getting *some* acting work.

- I'm gathering experience.

- I'm getting clearer about the work I really want.

- I do get to meet really interesting people.

- I've come a long way.

- I've had some really good auditions.

- I love the feeling of a really good audition.

   Result: (Vibrational relativity has improved.)

Contrasting Abundance Situation: My husband and I have both had jobs for years, and we saved some money—not a lot, but enough to live on for a year. We had a really great idea for our own business, and we had a friend who had enough money to help us get started, but now, after two years, we're still taking money from our savings to live on, and our savings account is going down fast. *I feel worried. I feel discouraged.*

   Resulting Desires: I want our business to really get going. I want dollars to flow powerfully into our business. I want our business to easily support a wonderful lifestyle.

   Resulting Emotions or Indications of Vibrational Discord: *I feel worried. I feel discouraged.* (There's a significant vibrational discord between my desire and my beliefs.)

   Deliberate Effort to Improve the Vibrational Relationship Between My New Desire and My Current Belief:

- I'm glad that we were able to open our business.

- I'm grateful that our friend believed in our vision.

- We're definitely making more money than we did at first.

- We'll figure out more what to do as we go along.

- Our current customers do appreciate us.

- I sure do appreciate our current customers.

  Result: (Vibrational relativity has improved.)

◦§◦§◦§ §◦§◦§◦

Chapter 28

My Money

Contrasting Abundance Situation: I never get ahead financially. It seems like unexpected things constantly come up, so I have to spend everything I make, and I have a lot of credit card debt, too, so I'm actually spending more than I'm making. I try to budget our expenses, but everything just costs so much. My wife works, and that helps, but as our kids get older, things cost more for them. *I feel worried. I feel discouraged.*

Resulting Desires: I want ample money to do the things I want and need to do. I want to get out of debt. I want to be able to do nice things for my family.

Resulting Emotions or Indications of Vibrational Discord: *I feel worried. I feel discouraged.* (There's a significant vibrational discord between my desire and my beliefs.)

Deliberate Effort to Improve the Vibrational Relationship Between My New Desire and My Current Belief:

- We do have a comfortable lifestyle.

- I can't think of anything that we really need that we don't have.

- We're living so much better than our parents did when they were our age.

- Our children rarely complain about any shortage.

- Our children are so eager about their lives.

- It's so rewarding to be a parent of children like these.

    Result: (Vibrational relativity has improved.)

Contrasting Defective-Car Situation: I've been working and saving since I got out of school, and I managed to save enough money for a big down payment on my car. I found a car that looked really good, and I paid over half down on it, so my payments are low. But I had the car for less than two months, and it started breaking down, so I had to borrow money to fix it. Now, the combination of my car payment and the repair costs adds up to more than if I had bought a brand-new car. *I feel blame. I feel discouraged. I feel anger.*

Resulting Desires: I want a new car. I want to receive fair value for the money I'm paying.

Resulting Emotions or Indications of Vibrational Discord: *I feel blame. I feel discouraged. I feel anger.* (There's a significant vibrational discord between my desire and my beliefs.)

Deliberate Effort to Improve the Vibrational Relationship Between My New Desire and My Current Belief:

- The repair shop *was* able to fix my car.

- I see no evidence now that it isn't running well.

- I'm glad I was able to find a way to get the money to fix it.

- I remember how excited I felt when I first saw this car.

- Right now, the car isn't different from my first sight of it.

- I do enjoy driving this car.

- This car was a good choice for me for now.

  Result: (Vibrational relativity has improved.)

Contrasting Financial-Security Situation: My husband and I have both worked our entire lives. We've always been very careful with our money, because we knew that at some point we would want to retire. We managed to accumulate a very nice nest egg. Our son, who works as a stockbroker, said we should let him invest it, and that we could really increase our savings for our retirement. So we gave him the money to manage, and now it's all gone—everything that we've worked for our whole lives. I don't see how we'll ever be able to retire. *I feel worried. I feel discouraged. I feel blame. I feel anger. I feel insecurity. I feel fear.*

  Resulting Desires: I want to feel financially secure. I want to be able to retire someday. I want to love and trust my son.

  Resulting Emotions or Indications of Vibrational Discord: *I feel worried. I feel discouraged. I feel blame. I feel anger. I feel insecurity. I feel fear.* (There's a significant vibrational discord between my desire and my beliefs.)

Deliberate Effort to Improve the Vibrational Relationship Between My New Desire and My Current Belief:

- Our son, whom I love dearly, really meant well.

- We weren't planning on retiring immediately anyway.

- I do enjoy the stimulation of my job, for now, in any case.

- There are so many wonderful aspects to our lives.

- Our future planning has served us in other ways, too.

Result: (Vibrational relativity has improved.)

Contrasting Debt Situation: Several credit-card companies sent me cards that were already approved for credit. All I had to do was call the number to activate the cards, and they were ready for use. I bought several things that I'd needed, until I'd used all the credit on the first card, and then I started using another card and another card. Now, I have so much debt that I can barely pay the minimum payments that are due. *I feel worried. I feel blame. I feel discouraged. I feel insecurity. I feel fear.*

Resulting Desires: I want more money so that I can pay my bills. I want to be out of debt. I want enough money to be able to afford the things I want and need.

Resulting Emotions or Indications of Vibrational Discord: *I feel worried. I feel blame. I feel discouraged. I feel insecurity. I feel fear.* (There's a significant vibrational discord between my desire and my beliefs.)

Deliberate Effort to Improve the Vibrational Relationship Between My New Desire and My Current Belief:

- It's nice that the credit-card companies trusted me.

- I've always prided myself in keeping my word.

- I did have a good time purchasing things I needed.

- My life is much more comfortable because of those things.

  Result: (Vibrational relativity has improved.)

Chapter 29

My World

Contrasting Strife-and-Starvation Situation: Our whole world is such a mess. There are so many wars, so much conflict, and so many people suffering . . . I don't understand why, when we have all this technology and so many resources, there are so many people who are still going hungry. It seems like we should have figured things out better by now. *I feel discouraged. I feel blame. I feel anger.*

Resulting Desires: I want everyone to have enough food. I want the people of the world to get along with each other.

Resulting Emotions or Indications of Vibrational Discord: *I feel discouraged. I feel blame. I feel anger.* (There's a significant vibrational discord between my desire and my beliefs.)

Deliberate Effort to Improve the Vibrational Relationship Between My New Desire and My Current Belief:

- Most of what is actually around me is harmonious.

- I rarely see people really starving or suffering around me.

- There's much more wellness in the world than sickness.

- There have probably always been conflicts in the world.

- The standard of life, worldwide, is definitely improving.

- For most of the world, things are getting better and better.

  Result: (Vibrational relativity has improved.)

Contrasting Planetary Situation: The planet seems unstable. There are so many earthquakes, mud-slides, tidal waves, and hurricanes that suddenly sweep in and cause destruction. I almost don't want my family to leave home for fear something will happen and we'll be separated from each other, be hurt, or even worse. *I feel worried. I feel insecurity. I feel fear.*

Resulting Desires: I want my family to be safe. I want us to live long, happy lives.

Resulting Emotions or Indications of Vibrational Discord: *I feel worried. I feel insecurity. I feel fear.* (There's a significant vibrational discord between my desire and my beliefs.)

Deliberate Effort to Improve the Vibrational Relationship Between My New Desire and My Current Belief:

- These things have been present all the days of my life.

- Usually, the majority of the people affected survive.

- People often receive enough warning to safely evacuate.

- We live on a changing earth, and it will always be so.

- It's easy to worry about things that have nothing to do with me.

  Result: (Vibrational relativity has improved.)

Contrasting Travel Situation: I feel so limited; I seem to be able to explore or understand only a tiny part of this world. There are so many places I'd like to visit, but I can't get enough time off from work to go very far, or to stay long enough to really discover anything. I feel like I'm missing out on so much. *I feel bored. I feel disappointed.*

Resulting Desires: I want to explore the world. I want to have broader, more expansive, experiences.

Resulting Emotions or Indications of Vibrational Discord: *I feel bored. I feel disappointed.* (There's a significant vibrational discord between my desire and my beliefs.)

Deliberate Effort to Improve the Vibrational Relationship Between My New Desire and My Current Belief:

- There's still plenty of time for me to find a way to travel.

- Right now it might be a good idea to gather information about the world.

- I think I'll make a list of the places I'd most like to see.

- There are some places that cost less than others to visit.

- It will be fun to make a long list of interesting destinations.

- It will be enjoyable, someday, to add to the list as I check things off.

Result: (Vibrational relativity has improved.)

Contrasting Environmental Situation: I'm afraid that we're destroying our planet. The air isn't clean anymore. You can't drink the water; it's poison. Fish are dying; the ice caps are melting. *I feel blame. I feel anger. I feel insecurity. I feel fear.*

Resulting Desires: I want our environment to be healthy. I want our planet to survive for the benefit of future generations.

Resulting Emotions or Indications of Vibrational Discord: *I feel blame. I feel anger. I feel insecurity. I feel fear.* (There's a significant vibrational discord between my desire and my beliefs.)

Deliberate Effort to Improve the Vibrational Relationship Between My New Desire and My Current Belief:

- Technology has provided wonderful filters for our drinking water.

- Much of our water is *not* polluted.

- Weather patterns have cycles that we tend to forget.

- While there are some polluted areas, other areas are not.

- I'm still breathing and drinking water, and I'm doing just fine.

- My worries about the planet could be unfounded.

Result: (Vibrational relativity has improved.)

ക്ക്ക് ട്ട്ട

Chapter 30

My Government

Contrasting Government Situation: I'm very tired of the inefficiency of governmental bureaucracy. There are so many government requirements that you have to hire people whom you shouldn't even need . . . just to fill out the bureaucratic forms. You can't even get the bureaucracy on the phone to personally answer a question. I've wasted so much of my time just trying to find out what I'm supposed to do so that I can do it the way they want it done the first time. We need a better bureaucratic system. *I feel frustration. I feel overwhelmed. I feel blame.*

Resulting Desires: I want an efficient government. I want the things that are required of me by my government to be easy for me to accomplish.

Resulting Emotions or Indications of Vibrational Discord: *I feel frustration. I feel overwhelmed. I feel blame.* (There's a significant vibrational discord between my desire and my beliefs.)

Deliberate Effort to Improve the Vibrational Relationship Between My New Desire and My Current Belief:

- In time, I always understand what's required of me.

- I'm capable of learning new procedures as things change.

- Organization is difficult when so many people are involved.

- All large organizations have to work at their communication skills.

- A government does have some viable purpose and advantages.

    Result: (Vibrational relativity has improved.)

Contrasting Government's Financial-Deficit Situation: Our government is so inefficient and ineffective. If it needs more money, it just arbitrarily takes it from us. There's no financial accountability; money is spent so foolishly, and then they complain that there isn't enough for the things that really matter to *us*. What a mess. I don't know how anyone could ever straighten it out. *I feel disappointment. I feel blame. I feel anger.*

Resulting Desires: I want my taxes to be used effectively and efficiently.

Resulting Emotions or Indications of Vibrational Discord: *I feel disappointment. I feel blame. I feel anger.* (There's a significant vibrational discord between my desire and my beliefs.)

Deliberate Effort to Improve the Vibrational Relationship Between My New Desire and My Current Belief:

- I don't really understand the economics of government.

- I couldn't easily direct those trillions of dollars.

- The government does continue to function.

- There are advantages to its functioning.

- If the government disappeared tomorrow, we would miss it.

- Government *does* provide some valuable stability.

  Result: (Vibrational relativity has improved.)

Contrasting National-Pride Situation: When I was a kid, I felt so passionate about my country. I was thrilled when I heard patriotic songs, and I loved to hear stories of things that had happened as our nation was forming and we were evolving. But I don't feel patriotic anymore; I guess I know too much now. I don't feel good about decisions my government is making. *I feel disappointment. I feel blame. I feel anger.*

Resulting Desires: I want to feel proud of my country.

Resulting Emotions or Indications of Vibrational Discord: *I feel disappointment. I feel blame. I feel anger.* (There's a significant vibrational discord between my desire and my beliefs.)

Deliberate Effort to Improve the Vibrational Relationship Between My New Desire and My Current Belief:

- My opinions aren't based on an in-depth study.
- I wouldn't want the job of running the government.
- I didn't personally know any of those historical leaders.
- I don't really know that things are any worse today.

Result: (Vibrational relativity has improved.)

Current Contrasting Citizens'-Freedom Situation:
It feels as if our personal freedoms are rapidly eroding. Our government seems to have gone crazy in using its strong-armed tactics under the guise of serving the "greater good." What about *my good?* What about the good of those like me? They've gone crazy. I know this wasn't what our Founding Fathers had in mind. They're probably rolling over in their graves. *I feel disappointment. I feel blame. I feel anger. I feel insecurity. I feel grief. I feel powerless.*

Resulting Desires: I want our current leaders to uphold the intentions of the wise founders of this nation. I want my freedoms, which were intended by the founders of this nation, to be upheld.

Resulting Emotions or Indications of Vibrational Discord: *I feel disappointment. I feel blame. I feel anger. I feel insecurity. I feel grief. I feel powerless.* (There's a significant vibrational discord between my desire and my beliefs.)

Deliberate Effort to Improve the Vibrational Relationship Between My New Desire and My Current Belief:

- No matter who's elected, my life is always pretty much the same.

- My decisions affect my life much more than theirs do.

- I'm able to experience freedom as I move about.

- The government doesn't stand in the way of my personal choices.

- I didn't know our Founding Fathers personally.

- Our Founding Fathers, had they remained here throughout everything that has transpired in the world, may have arrived at conclusions similar to those of our current government officials.

  Result: (Vibrational relativity has improved.)

Chapter 31

The Value of Improved Vibrational Relativity

Often, when considering the idea of being the creator of their own reality, people will argue that it is extremely difficult to be standing in the middle of a very much unwanted condition and at the same time offer more pleasant thoughts about their future experience. They argue that it would be so much easier to create a bright and beautiful future from a more pleasant *now* experience. We understand their thinking, and we do agree that it *is* easier to feel good under positive conditions than negative ones. Therefore, we understand people's wishes that things could have gone better for them before now so that *now* could be a happier launching pad for that which is still to come.

Some people feel deep resentment over the unpleasant facts of their earlier life experiences as they recount unpleasant details of unfairness, or even physical abuse, that took place during their childhood. They often feel defensive, and we do not argue with their right to feel that way. We often agree that under the conditions they have lived, their negative response is justified. But we also always add that even though they are justified in their negative response to what happened to them, still, that negative emotion indicates that they are holding themselves in a place where they cannot receive what they really desire.

Those words, however, usually only serve to annoy them further, for they feel the way they feel, and they have been practicing this position for so long that our words (even though very wise ones) do not dissuade them from their practiced belief about the injustices they have experienced.

Have You Been Creating Deliberately, or by Default?

Many of our physical friends feel a deep memory stirring when we explain to them that they are the creator of their reality. They *do* want to create their own reality. And many, in time, resonate with the idea that they are vibrationally based Beings living in a vibrationally based Universe. And often, they even accept the idea that they are born with an *Emotional Guidance System* within them that helps them know the content of their own personal vibrational offering, which helps them to know, at all times, if what they are in the process of creating will be pleasing to them when it arrives. *But most people, even those who consciously acknowledge their vibrational nature and <u>Emotional Guidance System</u>, still offer most of their vibrations—and therefore create most of their reality—by default. They do so because they offer most of their vibrations in response to the reality that they are observing rather than in response to the reality that they prefer.*

There is something so compelling about what has already materialized into your experience. You call it *reality;* you call it *fact;* you call it *evidence;* you call it *proof.* You document it in writing, and with pictures. You call it *history* . . . and in doing all of that, you overlook the absolutely temporary nature of it (whatever *it* is). From our point of view, you have allowed your "reality" to hold a more dominant place in your perception of life than it deserves, and by your ardent attention to your current "reality," you slow your progress to the reception of even more pleasing "now" experiences.

We would like you to understand that NOW is mostly only the platform from which you move into what is next. And LIFE is really about the MOVING into what is next. We want you to recall the delicious nature of focusing upon the SENSATION OF CREATING YOUR OWN REALITY rather than giving so much attention to the REALITY THAT YOU ARE CREATING. Can you feel the distinction?

You Are Traveling on Two Concurrent Journeys

We visited recently with a woman who was experiencing the severe discomfort of arthritic hips. Her current state of reality was one of nearly constant physical discomfort.

If we could just help her to understand that her painful physical condition is only the *temporary* place that she is currently standing, then she could begin to move to a better-feeling condition immediately. If we could just get her to focus upon WHERE she is MOVING TO instead of focusing upon the REALITY that is right now occurring. . . . If we could just get her to focus upon the SENSATION of MOVING TO a better-feeling place rather than focusing upon the REALITY that seems to have concluded—her situation would begin to improve immediately.

We wanted to help her see that there are two journeys running along concurrently in her experience: the *Action Journey* (or the reality of her painful arthritic hips), and the *Emotional Journey* (the emotion that she is choosing to feel) as she moves through her day.

From her current reality, or the platform from which she is now launching into her next experiences, she has these choices:

- She has painful arthritic hips and feels fear, anger, worry, blame, or despair.

- She has painful arthritic hips and feels *hope.*

You see, her current condition of painful hips is her *Action Journey.* That *is* happening. It *is* reality. That *is* her current condition. And we certainly can understand why it would have her attention. But if she could, just for a little while, try to focus upon her *Emotional Journey*—if she could just accept that her hips hurt for now and set that *Action Journey* aside in her mind for just a little while, and focus upon her *Emotional Journey* options, then her vibrational point of attraction would begin to change. And in doing that, her physical condition would begin to change.

You cannot continue to offer the same vibration that got you to where you are, and now get to someplace different. You have to do something different with your attention, with your focus, and with your vibration.

❧ ❧ ❧ ☙ ☙ ☙

Chapter 32

The *Action Journey* and the *Emotional Journey*

Focus on the idea of moving your physical body from one place to another. Maybe you are in your vehicle, on the highway, driving to another city, or walking down a trail in the woods with a backpack filled with food and supplies. In each example, you probably have a clear idea of your destination. You are purposely moving from one place to another with an intention of arriving somewhere. We will call this your *Action Journey* (your actual journey of action).

This actual journey can be described in very factual terms: You can identify the distance you plan to travel. You can describe the weather that is occurring. You can estimate, with fair accuracy, your estimated time of arrival.

There are many straightforward, easy-to-understand, quantifiable aspects to this *Action Journey* that you have embarked upon.

Now we want to call your attention to another part of your journey. And it is *this* perspective of your journey that actually sets the tone for everything that will subsequently happen in your life experience. For your journeys are not only the cut-and-dried factual experiences of moving from one place to another. They are much more about the way you *feel* as you travel. We call this aspect of your experiences your *Emotional Journey*.

So, we want you to understand that you are never only upon one of these journeys. In every moment, you are experiencing *two* concurrent journeys: your *Action Journey* (your awareness of time and space, and things already manifested) and your *Emotional Journey* (your vibrational response to your powerful moment in time, from which all future experiences are molded).

There are endless potential combinations of *Action Journeys* and *Emotional Journeys,* and we will offer some examples of those here. We want you to come to know that the most important aspect of any journey is the emotional aspect, for if you are aware of how you feel, and are able to affect those feelings deliberately, then (and only then) will you have conscious control of all future outcomes of your life experience. We call this *Deliberate Creation.*

On the other hand, if your dominant focus is upon the *Action Journey*—observing and responding to the things that are happening right now in your experience, allowing your feelings to naturally follow the patterns of your observations, and making no effort to guide your feelings but merely responding to conditions and circumstances . . . then you will have no conscious control of your own life experience. We call this *creating by default.*

ᦂ ᦂ ᦂ ᦂ ᦂ ᦂ

Chapter 33

Applying the *Book-of-Positive-Aspects* Process

Whatever you are focused on is causing an activation of a vibration within you, and the better you feel while you are focused, the more beneficial your focus is. Whenever you deliberately look for the positive aspects of something, you are deliberately activating beneficial vibrations. Now, it is not important that you find the perfect vibration, or the best vibration, but deliberately looking for the positive aspects of a subject will automatically get you pointed in the right direction.

Sometimes if something has been bothering you, it is not easy to write a long list (or even a short one) of its positive aspects. But whenever you are determined to find a positive aspect, you can usually find one. And once you find one and activate it within you, you can then find another and another, until, within a short 15 or 20 minutes of focusing upon a subject, you can significantly change your vibration on the subject.

The process is simple: Obtain a notebook that is comfortable to use, and write on the cover: MY BOOK OF POSITIVE ASPECTS. Open to the first page and write: POSITIVE ASPECTS OF . . . (and then write the subject for which you want improvement in your vibrational relationship). Then write your list of positive aspects on that subject.

Do not try to force these ideas, but let them flow easily through you onto your paper. Write as long as the thoughts flow, and then read what you have written and enjoy your own words. It can be helpful to focus on the situation and then ask yourself: "What do I like about you? What are your good points?"

*This process works best if your range on
the Emotional Guidance Scale is within the following:*

1. Joy/Knowledge/Empowerment/Freedom/ Love/Appreciation
2. Passion
3. Enthusiasm/Eagerness/Happiness
4. Positive Expectation/Belief
5. Optimism
6. Hopefulness
7. Contentment
8. Boredom
9. Pessimism
10. Frustration/Irritation/Impatience

If you are feeling much worse than this, then other processes may be more effective to help you improve your vibration relativity. But we have noticed that anyone with deliberate intent, regarding any subject, can improve the way they feel; and when they do, things must begin to improve in their experience. The *Law of Attraction* insists that it must!

Here are some examples of how the *Positive Aspects Process* could help you release resistance and improve the vibrational relativity between what is happening right now and what you would like to be happening:

Home-Deterioration Situation: I've lived in the same place for a long time, and I'm tired of it. It doesn't meet our needs at all anymore, but we can't really afford to move. I even find myself looking for excuses to not be at home because I don't feel good when I'm there. *I feel frustration. I feel irritation. I feel pessimism.*

Positive Aspects of My Current Ho

- My things have been in the same place enough that I know where they are.

- There is stability in being in a familiar

- We've fixed this place up as much as we intend to, so we can now spend our free time doing other things we like.

- Our friends and professional contacts are not likely to lose touch with us here.

- We have a good relationship with our mail carrier and other service people who have known us for a long time.

- It's been fun watching our landscaped yard mature. Some of those trees and shrubs are like old friends.

Co-worker Situation: I share an office with someone whom I can hardly stand to be around. She doesn't have a nice thing to say about much of anything, and she wants to talk all the time. She doesn't enjoy her job, and she treats me like I'm foolish when I want to do mine. I wish she'd either quit or get fired. Life is too short to have to spend so much time with someone so unpleasant. *I feel irritation. I feel blame. I feel anger.*

Positive Aspects of My Office Mate:

- I'm pleased that I have employment.

- I'm happy that I have a regular paycheck.

- I like the financial stability that my work provides.

- I enjoy many of the people who work here.

- My job requires focus, and I like the feeling of being productive.

- My office mate keeps a neat desk.

- She always dresses neatly.

- She has a great laugh.

- She has a good background in our field.

- She learns quickly.

Government Situation: I'm very tired of the inefficiency of governmental bureaucracy. There are so many government requirements that you have to hire people whom you shouldn't even need . . . just to fill out the bureaucratic forms. You can't even get the bureaucracy on the phone to personally answer a question. I've wasted so much of my time just trying to find out what I'm supposed to do so that I can do it the way they want it the first time. We need a better bureaucratic system. *I feel frustration. I feel overwhelmed. I feel blame.*

Positive Aspects of Government:

- I'm glad that the government tends to some of the things that I don't want to deal with.

- Our government employs many people, which adds beneficially to the economy.

- Our government and our laws provide a stable platform for us.

- There are some talented, progressive thinkers in our government.

- Those who comprise our government come and go.

As you read these examples, or even as you address issues in your own life experience, it is easy to get lost in an ideological debate over the correctness, rightness, actual truth, or facts of the issue. But there are many things that are true, things that someone, somewhere, has created that you do not want to create in your experience; and there are things from your own past that, even though they were true, you do not want to continue to repeat in your future.

When you care enough about something to actually take the time to make it an entry in your *Book of Positive Aspects,* it is certain that, with far less effort and energy than you would spend debating the truth or facts of an issue with someone, you can improve the relationship between the vibration of your desire and the vibration of your belief. This *Positive-Aspects Process* will give you an immediate vibrational improvement. . . . Enjoy your improved feeling; compliment yourself for improving your vibrational relativity; move on with your day; and the continued evidence of your accomplishment will, in time, reveal itself to you.

༝ᢀ ༝ᢀ ༝ᢀ ᢀ༝ ᢀ༝ ᢀ༝

Chapter 34

Applying the *Segment-Intending Process*

The process of *Segment Intending* is one whereby you define the vibrational characteristics of the time segment you are moving into. It is a way of prepaving your vibrational path, so to speak, for easier and more enjoyable travel. It will help you focus less on how things *are* feeling right now, and more upon how you *want* them to feel. It is a powerful process that emphasizes the *Emotional Journey,* while de-emphasizing the *Action Journey.*

This process will help you be more deliberate about focusing your thoughts. It will help you become more aware of where your thoughts currently are, and it will help you to more deliberately choose the thoughts that you offer. In time, it will feel very natural to you to stop, for a moment, upon entering a new segment, and deliberately direct your own intent or expectation.

You enter a new segment anytime your intentions change: If you are washing dishes and the telephone rings . . . you enter a new segment. When you get into your vehicle . . . you enter a new segment. When another person walks into the room . . . you enter a new segment.

If you will take the time to get your thought of your *expectation* for the segment started even before you are inside your new segment, then you will be able to set the tone of the segment more specifically than if you walk into the segment and begin to observe it as it already is. In other words, *Segment Intending* is focusing upon your *Emotional Journey,* not on the *Action Journey.*

Whenever you are setting forth your intentions about how you want to feel and how you would like a segment to unfold, it is always beneficial.

This process works best if your range on
the Emotional Guidance Scale is within the following:

4. Positive Expectation/Belief
5. Optimism
6. Hopefulness
7. Contentment
8. Boredom
9. Pessimism
10. Frustration/Irritation/Impatience
11. Overwhelment

Fatigue Situation: I have no energy. I feel tired all of the time. I can barely get through the day. I'm having a hard time keeping up with the things I need to do, and I'm not enjoying anything because I'm so tired. *I feel so overwhelmed.*

New Segment: I finished my day at work. I stopped at the grocery store and bought several bags of food and household items. I have now parked in my driveway, and I have turned off my vehicle, but before getting out of the car to begin unloading my groceries, I have decided to apply this process of *Segment Intending:*

This new segment involves: Moving the groceries from the car to the house, and putting them where they belong.

My intentions for this new segment: *During this segment, I want to feel efficient. I want to feel productive. I want to feel organized. I want to feel good in my body. I want to feel appreciation for the groceries, and I want to feel appreciation for my kitchen.*

Job Situation: I get paid pretty well, compared to a lot of other jobs around, but I don't look forward to going to work. I've been doing pretty much the same thing for a long time, and I don't feel stimulated at all. No one seems to notice what I do unless I make a mistake. The day goes by so slowly . . . and then I have to turn around and do it all again the next day. *I feel boredom. I feel pessimism.*

> **New Segment:** I've showered and dressed and have eaten breakfast. I've now driven to work and have just parked my car in the parking space. Before going inside, I've decided to sit in my car for two or three minutes to apply this process of *Segment Intending:*
>
>> **This new segment involves:** A one-hour staff meeting where my manager and everyone in her department will meet. We have this meeting every Monday morning.
>>
>>> **My intentions for this new segment:** *I want to be on time. I want it to be evident that my weekend has refreshed me. I want to feel clear-minded and happy. I want to enjoy the others who are gathering. I want this meeting to feel productive. I want to feel happy that I attended this meeting, and I want others to be happy that I was there.*

This *Segment-Intending Process* may feel too simple or too easy to be of value, but a deliberate application of this process will turn an unfocused life, filled with unsatisfying experiences, into a dynamic, passionate life experience.

This process improves the relationship between your current belief vibration and the vibration of your desire because it causes you to stop focusing on *what-is* and to begin focusing on something that is coming. With some practice, you can become very adept at increasing your positive expectation. When your negative emotion is as slight as the range we have just indicated here, it is not such a big vibrational leap for you to be more optimistic about your future experience. But if you are feeling stronger negative emotion than we have indicated as the range for this process, you may have a difficult time anticipating a positive upcoming segment, and you could just carry the negative feeling you are having right now on into the next segment, too. If you find yourself doing that, discontinue the process, for it is of no value, for you will only focus on what you *do not* want even more specifically into your future segment.

Be playful and hopeful as you begin this process, and in time you will feel powerful and certain as you deliberately instruct Universal Forces and the interplaying factors to behave in exactly the way you have intended. *With practice, this Segment-Intending Process will give you the sensation of being a masterful artist or creator who dictates all outcomes, who identifies all details, and who deliberately sculpts the details of your own life experience—for you are the creator of your own life experience.*

ᵃᵍ ᵃᵍ ᵃᵍ ᵍᵉ ᵍᵉ ᵍᵉ

Ch

App
Wouldn't-It-
Pr

The Amazing Power of Deliberate Int

6. Hopefulness
7. Contentm
8. Boredo
9. Pes
10.

Most people have been trained to be objective—meaning that they look at the pluses and minuses, the pros and the cons—but in considering both sides of things, they also activate the contradictory vibrations, which cause a hindering resistance to the allowing of what they desire. When you say, "I want this thing to happen, *but* it hasn't happened yet," you are not only activating the vibration of your desire, you are also activating a vibration of the *absence* of your desire—so nothing changes for you. And often, even when you do not speak the second part of the sentence and you only say, "I want this to happen," there is an unspoken vibration within you that continues to hold you in a state of not allowing your desire.

But when you say, "Wouldn't it be nice if this desire would come to me?" you achieve a different sort of expectation that is much less resistant in nature. The vibrational relativity between your desire and your belief is now much more in alignment.

This process works best if your range on
the Emotional Guidance Scale is within the following:

4. Positive Expectation/Belief
5. Optimism

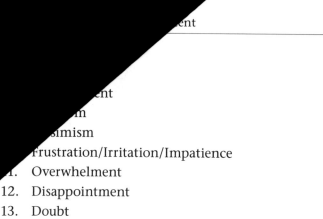

ent

m

imism

rustration/Irritation/Impatience

. Overwhelment

12. Disappointment

13. Doubt

14. Worry

15. Blame

16. Discouragement

Home-Space Situation: My home is a mess. It's so small, and it has such inadequate storage that I don't have anywhere to put anything. And even when I do try to clean it up to get more organized, I just make a bigger mess than before. *I feel frustration. I feel overwhelmed.*

Wouldn't it be nice if . . .

. . . I could find a handy place to put some of our things?

. . . I could get rid of some things we don't need and free up more space?

. . . we had an extra storage building in the backyard?

. . . my husband would sell the old car, leaving us more garage space?

. . . I could find a little time here and there to improve things?

. . . a really organized person could come to help me . . . or inspire me?

Home-Deterioration Situation: I've lived in the same place for a long time, and I'm tired of it. It doesn't meet our needs at all anymore, but we can't really afford to move. I even find myself looking for excuses to not be at home because I don't feel good when I'm there. *I feel frustration. I feel irritation. I feel pessimism.*

Wouldn't it be nice if . . .

. . . we could fix up the patio in the backyard?

. . . we could find great new furniture for the living room at a bargain price?

. . . we could get rid of the unneeded junk that's crowding our space?

. . . we found a great new place to live that's in our affordable price range?

. . . we could add a beautiful family room on the backside of the house?

. . . we could paint inside and out with wonderful, fresh new colors . . . ?

Neighbors' Situation: I used to like this neighborhood, but then some people moved in next door, and they're just awful neighbors. Their dog uses our yard for a bathroom, and they have three or four junker cars parked in their driveway instead of on the street in front of the house. I'm embarrassed to have people over to visit. *I feel blame. I discouraged. I feel anger.*

Wouldn't it be nice if . . .

. . . those neighbors would move someplace else?

. . . their dog found a bathroom he likes better?

. . . their dog could respond to the power of my mind?

. . . they were able to sell all of those old cars?

. . . I'm wrong about them and they're actually very nice to know?

. . . I could get so involved in my own yard that I wouldn't notice theirs so much?

Home-Maintenance Situation: Our house is costing us a fortune just to keep things working. It wasn't built very well to begin with, and now it's ten years old and things are constantly breaking down. Every time I turn around, something else needs to be repaired. *I feel frustrated. I feel overwhelmed. I feel disappointed. I feel discouraged.*

Wouldn't it be nice if . . .

. . . we could find a great repairman?

. . . that was the last thing that would break for a while?

. . . the things that we buy would last longer?

. . . we could buy good-quality things that would last longer?

. . . we could just relax and accept that things are constantly coming and going?

. . . our income and would get bigger and bigger?

Adult-Child Situation: I have an adult daughter who's always mad at me. No matter how much time I spend with her, it's never enough. When I *am* with her, she spends most of our time complaining about how we don't spend enough time together! I'm so busy, and I don't have much time to spend with her, but it's really not fun to be with her because of the way she feels. *I feel guilty. I feel angry. I feel disappointed.*

Wouldn't it be nice if . . .

. . . we could find a little more time to have fun together?

. . . we could chat briefly every day and catch up on everything?

. . . I could see her great smile more often?

. . . her life was filled with things *she* loves to do?

. . . her life felt full, rewarding, and wonderful to her?

. . . we could always make each other feel great?

Marital Situation: I still love my wife, but our relationship is nothing like it used to be. When we were first married, I couldn't wait to see her at the end of the day; and now, to be honest, I sort of dread going home. She complains a lot about so many different things, and I think she blames me for everything that isn't going the way she wants it to. I don't want to leave, but it's sure not fun staying, either. *I feel frustration. I feel blame. I feel irritation.*

Wouldn't it be nice if . . .

. . . we could feel the way we did when we first met?

. . . I just couldn't wait to get home to be with her?

. . . she could find some things that she truly loves to do?

. . . we could both lighten up and have more fun?

. . . she could just let go of the things that bother her?

. . . we could always be each other's best friend?

Meddling-Parent Situation: I haven't lived at home for over ten years, but my mother still thinks that she needs to tell me what to do, so I avoid her because I don't like being bossed around. And then she gets mad, and that's even worse. But when we're together, she treats me like I don't know how to live my own life. *I feel blame. I feel anger.*

Wouldn't it be nice if . . .

. . . my mother could find a compelling new hobby?

. . . one of her friends could inspire something different in her?

. . . she could realize that I'm a really responsible person?

. . . I didn't let her bother me so much?

. . . I could just love her so much I wouldn't notice her meddling?

. . . we only got together when we're both really happy?

Debt Situation: Several credit-card companies sent me cards that were already approved for credit. All I had to do was call the number to activate the cards, and they were ready for use. I bought several things that I'd needed until I had used all the credit on the first card, and then I started using another card, and another. . . . Now I have so much debt that I can't even pay the minimum payments that are due. *I feel worried. I feel blame. I feel discouraged. I feel insecurity. I feel fear.*

Wouldn't it be nice if . . .

. . . I were debt free?

. . . I could pay my cards off every month?

. . . I could find lower interest-rate cards?

. . . I could pay them off and keep only a couple for convenience?

. . . I could find a way to make some extra money?

. . . a solution I haven't considered would appear and solve my problem?

Strife-and-Starvation Situation: Our whole world is such a mess. There are so many wars, so much conflict, and so many people suffering. I don't understand why, when we have all this technology and so many resources, there are so many people who are still hungry. It seems like we should have figured things out better by now. *I feel discouraged. I feel blame. I feel anger.*

Wouldn't it be nice if . . .

. . . we could help each other more?

. . . people could feel their own power?

. . . our tax dollars could be used more productively?

. . . everyone had enough to eat?

. . . everyone could be happy?

. . . we could respect each other's differences?

Government Situation: I'm very tired of the inefficiency of governmental bureaucracy. There are so many government requirements that you have to hire people whom you shouldn't even need . . . just to fill out the bureaucratic forms. You can't even get the bureaucracy on the phone to personally answer a question. I've wasted so much of my time just trying to find out what I'm supposed to do so that I can do it the way they want it the first time. We need a better bureaucratic system. *I feel frustration. I feel overwhelmed. I feel blame.*

Wouldn't it be nice if . . .

. . . we could devise a more efficient bureaucratic system?

. . . I could hire someone who understands this, who could do it for me?

. . . through experience, they would find a better way?

. . . new technology could help us out?

. . . a whole new way of record keeping could be developed?

. . . the solution were right around the corner?

Government's Financial-Deficit Situation: Our government is so inefficient and ineffective. If it needs more money, it just arbitrarily takes it from us. There's no financial accountability; money is spent so foolishly, and then they complain that there isn't enough for the things that really matter to *us*. What a mess. I don't know how anyone could ever straighten it out. *I feel disappointment. I feel blame. I feel anger.*

Wouldn't it be nice if . . .

. . . someone with a wonderful financial background and insight would show up?

. . . the pendulum would swing in a more efficient direction?

. . . I had so much money that it didn't matter to me how money is spent?

. . . we were all thriving financially?

. . . everyone would do their part?

. . . we could find some talented leaders with a new economic approach?

As you move through your day, many different situations arise that cause the activation of a variety of vibrations within you. You feel good about some things, not so good about some other things, and some things you feel bad about. This *Wouldn't-It-Be-Nice-If . . . ? Process* can help you feel better almost every time if you are willing to focus in a better-feeling direction.

Saying the words, *Wouldn't It Be Nice if . . . ?* cues you up for an improved vibration and inspires deliberate focus. Saying these words also begins a positive activation even before you say the rest of the words that are related to the topic.

If you will deliberately play this game as you drive or while you are standing in line, or anytime that your attention does not need to be on something else, the vibrational relativity between your desire and your beliefs on a myriad of subjects will improve—and desires that are being held out there for you in vibrational escrow will begin showing up in your experience.

A consistent playing of this game will cause a gradual improvement in the vibrational relationship between where you are and where you want to be regarding every area of your life. This *Wouldn't-It-Be-Nice-If . . . ?* process is playfully, deceptively, and amazingly powerful.

⊰ ⊰ ⊰ ⊱ ⊱ ⊱

Chapter 36

Applying the
Which-Thought-Feels-Better? Process

T his process works best if you can sit for a few minutes and write your thoughts down on paper. In time, when you have played the game sufficiently, you will find success with it just by rolling the thoughts across your mind. But writing them down on paper causes a much more powerful point of focus, which makes it easier for you to *feel* the direction of your chosen thought.

To begin: First, write some brief statements of how you *feel* about the subject right now. *You could describe what has happened, but what is most important is that you describe how you feel.* (This will help you more easily recognize any improvement as you move through the process.)

Once you have written a few statements that indicate how you really feel right now, make this statement to yourself: *I'm going to reach for some thoughts about this subject that feel a little better.* Then, write a series of brief thoughts that come to your mind that might help you feel better about the subject. (At the conclusion of each statement, evaluate whether it feels better, the same, or worse than when you initially began.)

By focusing—with the intent of improving the way you feel about these subjects—you will improve the vibrational relationship between your desires and your beliefs; and then, in time, these situations must improve. *Your manifestations always follow the direction of your vibration: When you feel better, things improve. Every time.*

This process works best if your range on the <u>Emotional Guidance Scale</u> is within the following:

4. Positive Expectation/Belief
5. Optimism
6. Hopefulness
7. Contentment
8. Boredom
9. Pessimism
10. Frustration/Irritation/Impatience
11. Overwhelment
12. Disappointment
13. Doubt
14. Worry
15. Blame
16. Discouragement
17. Anger

Physical-Decline Situation: I worry that my body is deteriorating. I don't have the energy that I once had, and I can't do the things I used to enjoy doing. I have aches and pains, my knees hurt when I walk, and I don't dare try to run anymore. I'm scared that it's going to get worse and worse. *I feel worried.*

I'm going to reach for some thoughts about this subject that feel a little better:

- I should walk more often, but I can't make myself do it. (same)

- I could take a short walk and turn back anytime I feel like it. (better)

- I don't have enough energy to take a walk. (worse)

- If I walk a little every day, I could get stronger. (better)

- In time, I might enjoy my walks again. (better)
- I don't have to run the marathon today. (better)
- I can choose how far and how fast I walk. (better)
- But when I walk, my knees hurt. (worse)
- If I take it slow, it'll probably be all right. (better)
- My body has responded to exercise before. (better)
- I haven't exercised in a long time. (worse)
- If I decide to walk a little every day, I can do it. (better)
- I think I'll give it a try. (better)
- I hope I begin feeling better soon. (better)
- It will be nice to feel strong and vital again. (better)

Acting-Career Situation: I've wanted to be an actress since I was a little girl. I took some classes and found out that I'm pretty good at it. I get some acting work from time to time, but nothing exciting, and nothing that I really want. It's hard. There are so many people applying for the same work that I am that it seems hopeless. Maybe I should just forget about it and go get a real job. *I feel disappointed. I feel discouraged.*

I'm going to reach for some thoughts about this subject that feel a little better:

- I'm tired of going for auditions and not getting the part. (worse)
- I don't know what I should do differently. (worse)
- I don't understand why that person *did* get the part. (worse)
- I'm getting *some* acting experience. (better)
- I now understand the process involved in an audition. (better)

- I don't feel so frightened now when I audition. (better)

- Even famous actresses have gone through this. (better)

- If they survived it, I can, too. (better)

- It's going to feel so good to get a great acting part. (better)

- I know I can rise to whatever they need. (better)

- When I look back, I see great progress. (better)

- I'm just going to relax and try to have more fun. (better)

Defective-Car Situation: I've been working and saving since I got out of school, and I managed to save enough money for a big down payment on my car. I found a car that looked really good, and I paid over half down on it, so my payments are low. But I had the car for less than two months, and it started breaking down, so I had to borrow money to fix it. Now, the combination of my car payment and the repair costs adds up to more than if I had bought a brand-new car. *I feel blame. I feel discouraged. I feel anger.*

I'm going to reach for some thoughts
about this subject that feel a little better:

- It's so unfair. (worse)

- They knew the car was defective when they sold it to me. (worse)

- They're not ethical. (worse)

- At least the car is running well now. (better)

- It has caused me a lot of grief. (worse)

- If I just look at the car, I do like it. (better)

- I'm making the payments all right. (better)
- We do learn through experience. (better)
- I've complained about it enough. I think I'll move on. (better)

Financial-Security Situation: My husband and I have both worked our entire lives. We've always been very careful with our money, because we knew that at some point we would want to retire. We managed to accumulate a very nice nest egg. Our son, who works as a stockbroker, said we should let him invest it, and that we could really increase our savings for our retirement. So we gave him the money to manage, and now it's all gone—everything that we've worked for our whole lives. I don't see how we'll ever be able to retire. *I feel worried. I feel discouraged. I feel blame. I feel anger. I feel insecurity. I feel fear.*

I'm going to reach for some thoughts
about this subject that feel a little better:

- How could we have been so stupid? (worse)
- Our son should not have gambled with our money. (worse)
- His supervisor should have insisted on diversification. (worse)
- We will survive. (better)
- We aren't ready for retirement anyway. (better)
- We do still have our incomes. (better)
- We weren't using that money anyway. (better)
- We always cope with whatever is happening. (better)
- We'll figure it out. (better)
- We still have some time to figure it out. (better)

Planetary Situation: The planet seems unstable. There are so many earthquakes, mudslides, tidal waves, and hurricanes that suddenly sweep in and cause destruction. I almost don't want my family to leave home for fear something will happen and we'll be separated from each other, be hurt, or even worse. *I feel worried. I feel insecurity. I feel fear.*

*I'm going to reach for some thoughts
about this subject that feel a little better:*

- It would be awful to be involved in one of these tragedies. (worse)

- It's so frightening to think of the possibilities. (worse)

- I've lived many years and haven't experienced these things. (better)

- Our technology continues to improve to let us know in advance. (better)

- My children are all alert and deliberate about what they do. (better)

- None of us have experienced personal tragedy. (better)

- Worry isn't a productive use of my time. (better)

Environmental Situation: I'm afraid that we're destroying our planet. The air isn't clean anymore. You can't drink the water; it's poison. Fish are dying; the ice caps are melting. *I feel blame. I feel anger. I feel insecurity. I feel fear.*

*I'm going to reach for some thoughts
about this subject that feel a little better:*

- We've got to take better care of our planet. (worse)

- People are so selfish and not willing to do what needs to be done. (worse)

- I visited the town I grew up in, and I saw that very little had changed. (better)

- Some areas are more polluted than others. (better)
- That was true 50 years ago, also. (better)
- We're now more aware, and emission standards have been set. (better)
- Things are beginning to turn around. (better)
- There's always a great deal of evidence of Well-Being. (better)

Government's Financial-Deficit Situation: Our government is so inefficient and ineffective. If it needs more money, it just arbitrarily takes it from us. There's no financial accountability, money is spent so foolishly, and then they complain that there isn't enough for the things that really matter to *us*. What a mess. I don't know how anyone could ever straighten it out. *I feel disappointment. I feel blame. I feel anger.*

I'm going to reach for some thoughts
about this subject that feel a little better:

- If a business behaved that way, it would be bankrupt. (worse)
- It's obvious that they have no idea what they're doing. (worse)
- I'm better off today than I was ten years ago. (better)
- I'm better off today than I was even five years ago. (better)
- I'm not really affected much by their actions. (better)
- If I got personally involved, I might feel more tolerant. (worse)
- It's not my job to sort this out. (better)
- I think I'll focus on the things I *can* do something about. (better)

National-Pride Situation: When I was a kid, I felt so passionate about my country. I was thrilled when I heard patriotic songs, and I loved to hear stories of things that happened as our nation was forming and we were evolving. But I don't feel patriotic anymore; I guess I know too much now. I don't feel good about the decisions my government is making. *I feel disappointment. I feel blame. I feel anger.*

I'm going to reach for some thoughts
about this subject that feel a little better:

- The foreign-affairs policies of my government are frightening. (worse)

- I can't agree with the actions taken by my government. (worse)

- I'm embarrassed by some of the behavior exhibited by my President. (worse)

- I still believe in the ideals this nation was founded upon. (better)

- I can discern the distinction between those ideals and one man. (better)

- When something is really wrong, in time the tide always turns. (better)

- Everyone operates from their own vantage point of belief. (better)

- I get to choose for myself. (better)

- I still believe in our nation. (better)

- There's no place I'd rather live. (better)

- My own actions represent me. (better)

This *Which-Thought-Feels-Better? Process* gets right to the heart of vibrational relativity. When you play this game, you are utilizing your *Emotional Guidance System* in the most conscious way possible. You are deliberately making a statement, noticing how it feels, and then choosing another statement with the intent of improving the feeling. This process is really what *Deliberate Creating* is all about.

It takes no effort to just observe what is already before you, and there is no effort involved in considering any thought that just drifts into your mind, but it does require effort to *deliberately* choose what you are thinking about. And when you make those choices, based upon how each one feels in relationship with the one you have just been thinking, you can now close the vibrational gap between where you are and where you want to be—and the manifestation will soon follow. This is really *Deliberate Creating* at its best.

∾ᢒᢒᢒ ᢒᢒᢒ∾

Chapter 37

Applying the *Wallet Process*

We want you to remember that *what* you are currently living is not nearly as important as how you *feel* about what you are living, because what you are living is changing constantly. Some people, as they read those words, immediately take issue with them, for they believe that things are not changing—at least not for them.

If you feel as if things are not changing, or changing very slowly, this is the reason: You are giving most of your attention to the *what-is* you are living, and little of your attention to the *what-you-would-like-to-be-living*.

Because money is a big part of your day-to-day experience, a slight adjustment in the vibrational relationship between your desire and what you usually activate around the subject can make a very big difference in your experience. If it is your desire to have more money, but whenever you think about money you feel worried or frustrated, your *Emotional Guidance System* is indicating that you are moving in the wrong direction. You have to improve the vibrational relationship between your desire and the thoughts you most often think about this subject before things can change. And, as with all things, an improvement in the way you feel means that you are heading in the direction of your desire.

It is natural for abundance to flow easily into your experience, and the *Wallet Process* will help you offer a vibration that is compatible with your receiving of money instead of your pushing it away.

This process works best if your range on the Emotional Guidance Scale is within the following:

6. Hopefulness
7. Contentment
8. Boredom
9. Pessimism
10. Frustration/Irritation/Impatience
11. Overwhelment
12. Disappointment
13. Doubt
14. Worry
15. Blame
16. Discouragement

Wallet Process: First, obtain a $100 bill and put it in your wallet or purse. Keep it with you at all times, and whenever you hold your wallet or purse, remember that your $100 bill is there. Feel pleased that it is there, and remind yourself often of the added sense of security that it brings you.

Now, as you move through your day, take note of the many things that you could purchase with that hundred dollars. By holding the $100 bill and not spending it right away, you receive the vibrational advantage of it every time you even *think* about it. In other words, if you were to remember your hundred dollars and spend it on the first thing you noticed, you would receive the benefit of really *feeling* your financial well-being only once. But if you *mentally* spent that hundred dollars 20 or 30 times in that day, you will have received the vibrational *feeling* advantage of having spent two or three thousand dollars.

Each time you acknowledge that you have the power, right there in your wallet, to purchase this, or to do that, you add to your sense of financial well-being over and over again, and so your point of attraction begins to shift: *I could have that. I could have that. I have the ability to purchase that. . . .*

And, because you really *do* have the means to do just that (you are not pretending something that is not), there is now no hindering doubt or disbelief muddying the waters of your financial flow. The *Wallet Process* is a simple but powerful process—and it will change your financial point of attraction.

Read the *Current Contrasting Financial-Abundance Situation* in the following example and see if you can identify the vibrations of resistance that are preventing any improvement for the people in the example. Then, as you read the examples offered of a deliberate application of the *Wallet Process,* see if you can feel the vibrational shift.

Current Contrasting Financial-Abundance Situation: My husband and I have both had jobs for years, and we saved some money—not a lot, but enough to live on for a year. We had a really great idea for our own business, and we had a friend who had enough money to help us get started, but now, after two years, we're still taking money from our savings to live on, and our savings account is going down, fast. *I feel worried. I feel discouraged.*

Wallet Process: We've decided to take a drive. Each of us has in our possession $100. It's our plan, in the next hour or so, to drive to the commercial district near our home and *mentally* spend these very real dollars again and again. Whenever either of us sees something that we want, we're going to experience the fun of *mentally* purchasing it. After all, we've got the money, right here, right now, so we really *could* purchase an item if we wanted to. We're just going to drive around, look out the window, see what catches our attention, and *mentally buy* it if it pleases us.

- Let's have dinner there tonight. I love eating there.

- Let's stop at the flower stand and get a gigantic bouquet.

- I think I'll buy that outdoor cooker for our patio.

- Let's get that swing set for the grandkids.

- Let's place an order with the man selling firewood so we're ready for our first fire.

- I'm going to schedule a day at the spa.

- I'm going to get a great haircut.

- I think I'll stop and pick up some new shoes.

- Me, too.

- I love that rug! What a good price that is!

- I'd like two of three of those big garden flower pots.

- I'd like those outdoor tree lights.

- Let's get a new mailbox.

- And mulch for the front flower beds.

- I'm going to have the car washed and detailed.

- I love that rocking chair. Let's get it for the porch.

- How about new garden hoses. . . .

When you play this game the first time, it is possible that in identifying things that you *want* to purchase, you may activate your *feeling of not enough money,* so in the first minutes of the game, you may feel an increase in your discomfort rather than an increased feeling of relief. But as you play the game, if, with each item that you identify, you will stop and acknowledge, *Yes, if I really wanted to, I do have the money, right here, right now, to make this purchase,* your discomfort will soften. And as you play the game longer, that discomfort will go away altogether. And once the discomfort is gone, the resistance is gone. And when the resistance is gone . . . your financial situation must begin to improve.

ᦉᦉᦉ ᦀᦀᦀ

Chapter 38

Applying the *Focus-Wheel Process*

The *Focus Wheel* is perhaps the most powerful process we offer to assist you in quickly improving the vibrational relationship between your current *beliefs* and your current *desires*. As you experience this *Focus-Wheel Process,* you can actually feel the improvement taking place in the vibrational alignment of your Energies.

Imagine standing next to a playground merry-go-round, and it is your intention to jump up onto it. But it is going so fast that when you try to get on, you cannot. The difference in the momentum of the merry-go-round and your own is too great, so you just get knocked off into the bushes. But if the merry-go-round were to slow down, at some point you could jump right up onto it, and then when it speeds up, you can easily stay onboard.

A similar thing happens when there is a variation in the momentum of your desire and the momentum of your belief. Either your desire has to slow down or your belief has to speed up in order for alignment to occur.

By focusing on this process, you can slow the vibrational momentum of your desire enough so that you can get onboard, and then once you are on, you can increase the speed of the vibration.

This Focus Wheel process works best if your range on the <u>Emotional Guidance Scale</u> is within the following:

8. Boredom
9. Pessimism
10. Frustration/Irritation/Impatience
11. Overwhelment
12. Disappointment
13. Doubt
14. Worry
15. Blame
16. Discouragement
17. Anger

Now here's how to begin the *Focus-Wheel Process:* Draw a large circle on a sheet of paper. Then draw a smaller circle, about two inches in diameter, in the center of the large circle. Now sit back and look at the small circle and feel your eyes focus upon it.

Then, close your eyes for a moment and turn your attention to whatever has happened that has produced the negative emotion within you—and identify exactly what it is that you do *not* want.

Now say to yourself, *Well, I clearly know what I <u>don't</u> want. What is it that I <u>do</u> want?*

It is helpful if you try to identify what you do *not* want as well as what you *do* want in terms of the way you want to *feel* about it. Now write a brief statement of what you *do* want in the small circle in the center of your page.

Next, try to write statements around the outside edge of your large circle that match what you *do* want. When you find a statement that is a close enough match, you will know it. In other words, you will *feel* whether your statement does not match and throws you off the wheel into the bushes, so to speak, or whether it is a statement that is close enough to your desire that it now sticks.

The reason the *Focus-Wheel Process* is so effective is because the statements you are writing are those that you have deliberately chosen. They are general statements that you already believe, which *match* your desire. The reason it works is because the *Law of Attraction* is so very powerful that when you hold a thought for as little as 17 seconds, another thought like it will join it; and once those two thoughts come together, there is a combustion that occurs that makes your thoughts even more powerful.

As you find additional thoughts that feel good, continue writing them around the perimeter of your larger circle. Start at what 12 o'clock would be if you were looking at a clock, and then continue around to 1 o'clock, 2 o'clock, and so on, until you have 12 statements that feel good to you.

(Now, after writing on the 11:00 position, emphatically circle the words that you originally wrote in the center of your *Focus Wheel,* and notice that you do feel a closer vibrational alignment with that thought, when only minutes before, you were nowhere near that vibration.)

Fatigue Situation: I have no energy. I feel tired all of the time. I can barely get through the day. I'm having a hard time keeping up with the things I need to do, and I'm not enjoying anything because I'm tired all the time. *I feel overwhelmed.*

My statement of what I *don't* want: *I don't want to feel tired.*

My statement of what I *do* want: *I want to feel strong, hearty, and energized.*

My first attempt to get on the wheel (you can feel if you get thrown off into the bushes, and you can feel if your statement is close enough to your desire that you actually get on): *I've got to get control of myself.* (not on)

I can't go on like this. (not on)

I do remember feeling better than I feel right now. (on)

(That statement was close enough in vibrational relationship to your desire that it sticks. So write it on your focus wheel at the 12 o'clock position. And as you find other statements that stick, continue to write them around the clock, so to speak, at 1 o'clock, 2 o'clock and so on.)

I usually am hearty. (1 o'clock)

I do like feeling good. (2 o'clock)

(Your focus has now caused enough improvement in the vibrational relationship between where you are and where you want to be that you can now easily stay on the wheel. So make the most of it, and keep going. The more statements you make that are a vibrational match to your desire, the more you will stabilize in this new and improved vibration.)

My body is responsive. (3 o'clock)

I'm feeling better already. (4 o'clock)

Every day I'll feel stronger. (5 o'clock)

I look forward to talking walks again. (6 o'clock)

It's refreshing to deliberately get outside every day. (7 o'clock)

This is a beautiful day. (8 o'clock)

I have a very good body. (9 o'clock)

I like feeling good. (10 o'clock)

There are so many things I enjoy doing. (11 o'clock)

(This game has caused you to focus on the *feeling* of the vibrational variance between where you are and where you want to be, and in this short time, your vibrational relativity has improved tremendously—so much, in fact, that you can now write a statement in the small circle in the center of your focus wheel from where you are vibrationally right now—which matches your statement of desire): *I feel strong, hearty, and energized!*

Loneliness Situation: I don't have many friends. Really, I don't even have one really close friend, and it's not much fun going through life alone. I've had friendships in the past, but nothing that really clicked. It seems as if people are just looking for what they can get out of me, but then they don't really want to give anything back to me. *I feel discouraged. I feel lonely.*

My statement of what I *don't* want: *I don't want to be alone.*

My statement of what I *do* want: *I want to find a really good friend.*

My first attempt to get on the wheel (you can feel if you get thrown off into the bushes, and you can feel if your statement is close enough to your desire that you actually get on): *A good friend is hard to find.* (not on)

I have never had a really good friend. (not on)

I see other people who have good relationships. (on)

(That statement was close enough to the vibrational range of your desire, so write it at the 12 o'clock spot on the wheel.)

I've met some people whom I enjoy being with. (1 o'clock)

This isn't something that I should try to force into being. (2 o'clock)

I will know immediately when I meet someone I'd like to know better. (3 o'clock)

Usually when I really like someone, they usually like me, too. (4 o'clock)

(Your resistance has now subsided a great deal. Your vibrational relationship has really improved, so keep going. . . .)

I really haven't been trying very hard to meet anyone. (5 o'clock)

There are nice people all around. (6 o'clock)

There are others looking for relationships, too. (7 o'clock)

As I feel better, others who feel good will begin to show up. (8 o'clock)

There are many ways to meet new people. (9 o'clock)

I do like being with people. (10 o'clock)

This feels like a new beginning. (11 o'clock)

(You are now in alignment, so write the following in the center circle): *I'm excited about my new friends who are on the way to me.*

Co-worker Situation: I share an office with someone whom I can hardly stand to be around. She doesn't have a nice thing to say about much of anything, and she wants to talk all the time. She doesn't enjoy her job, and she treats me like I'm foolish when I want to do mine. I wish she'd either quit or get fired. Life is too short to have to spend so much time with someone so unpleasant. *I feel irritation. I feel blame. I feel anger.*

My statement of what I *don't* want: *I don't want to share space with someone so unpleasant.*

My statement of what I *do* want: *I want to spend my time with people who are nice to be with.*

My first attempt to get on the wheel (you can feel if you get thrown off into the bushes, and you can feel if your statement is close enough to your desire that you actually get on): *I wish she would get fired.* (not on)

I wish one of us could get transferred. (not on)

I like feeling good at work. (on)

(That statement was close enough in vibrational relationship to your desire that it sticks. So write it on your focus wheel at the 12 o'clock position.)

I do enjoy a lot of what I do at work all day. (1 o'clock)

I'm good at what I do at work. (2 o'clock)

(Your vibration is much better already, so make the most of it, and keep going until this better vibration and the good feelings really dominate.)

I like to show myself that I have the ability to focus.
(3 o'clock)

Often, when I'm very clear minded, others follow my lead.
(4 o'clock)

It won't hurt me to work on setting a good example. (5 o'clock)

She must have a strong desire. (6 o'clock)

I really don't know everything that my office mate is dealing with. (7 o'clock)

I'm fortunate that my life is going so well. (8 o'clock)

Most of my friends are great to be around. (9 o'clock)

If I try, I can get along with most people. (10 o'clock)

I'm willing to make a stronger effort for harmony. (11 o'clock)

(And in the center circle, now write): *I'm looking forward to our improved relationship.*

Acting-Career Situation: I've wanted to be an actress since I was a little girl. I took some classes and found out that I'm pretty good at it. I get some acting work from time to time, but nothing exciting, and nothing that I really want. It's hard. There are so many people applying for the same work that I am that it seems hopeless. Maybe I should just forget about it and go get a real job. *I feel disappointed. I feel discouraged.*

My statement of what I *don't* want: *I don't want to work so hard and get no results.*

My statement of what I *do* want: *I want to get a great acting part.*

My first attempt to get on the wheel (you can feel if you get thrown off into the bushes, and you can feel if your statement is close enough to your desire that you actually get on): *I go to an audition nearly every day.* (not on)

Someone out there will surely want to hire me. (not on)

That one audition last week was really interesting. (on)

(Your vibrational relativity is close enough now to get you on the wheel, so write that one at 12 o'clock.)

I like it when I get to meet interesting people. (1 o'clock)

I could feel that I was relaxed and that I did a good job. (2 o'clock)

It's all right if I'm not a match for a particular job. (3 o'clock)

I really only want to be chosen if I'm a really good match. (4 o'clock)

Many well-known actors have stood right where I'm standing. (5 o'clock)

Every audition gives me more great experience. (6 o'clock)

I've done enough auditions that my fear has now vanished. (7 o'clock)

I can feel that I'm getting closer and closer. (8 o'clock)

I can feel my confidence increasing with each interview. (9 o'clock)

I think I'm getting good at this. (10 o'clock)

I love being an actress. (11 o'clock)

(The vibration of your desire and your belief in this moment are now matching. So write the next statement in the center circle): *I will so enjoy these great parts coming my way.*

After focusing on something unwanted for a while and therefore activating vibrations that are not a match to what you really want, it becomes increasingly difficult to then turn your attention to what you want. But you must find a way to focus your attention differently in order to be able to *create* something different. This *Focus-Wheel Process* has been designed for that very reason. It helps you to jump in, from right where you are, and then spin yourself to higher and higher vibrations. This process will move you from great resistance to no resistance faster than any other.

The key to the power of this process is contained within its name: *Focus*. Whenever you take the time to focus upon something and write it on paper, your focus (and power) increases. The process of drawing the large circle emphasizes your deliberate intent to focus, and then, stating where you currently are in the beginning amplifies the vibrational discord that is currently present. It requires more focus, still, just to get on the wheel the first time; that is the moment of the biggest vibrational shift. But once your first statement has been written at the 12 o'clock position, less focus is required to stay there; and as you add another statement and another and another, your vibration stabilizes, and the vibrational relationship between your desire and your belief improves.

We would use this process on every subject that matters to us. We would use it to improve situations, to improve relationships, to attract more money, and to achieve improved bodily conditions. . . . This is a process worth learning and applying. It can transform your life.

ക§ ക§ ക§ ৡ৯ ৡ৯ ৡ৯

Chapter 39

Applying the
Finding-the-Feeling-Place
Process

The *Finding-the-Feeling-Place Process* is most helpful in making sure that you are radiating a vibration that will serve you, in that this is a process that will help you realize what you are actually attracting. This process is one of using your imagination to pretend that your desire has already come about and that you are now actually living the details of that desire.

As you focus upon what it feels like to be living your desire, you cannot, at the same time, be feeling the absence of your desire. So, with practice, you can tip the scale, so to speak, so that even though your desire has not yet actually manifested, you are offering a vibration as if it has—and then it *must*.

Your goal, in this process, is to conjure up images that cause you to offer a vibration that *allows* your desire. Your goal is to create images that *feel* good to you; your goal is to find the *feeling-place* of what it would be like to *have* your desire rather than finding the *feeling-place* of what it is like to *not* have it.

You could use a remembering technique, and *remember* a time more like that which you now desire; you could use an imagining technique *and imagine* or *pretend* that it is happening now, or you could focus upon someone who is already living your desire—and as you focus upon details of the desire that you hold, its vibrational essence within you will be activated. You do not have to be actually living something in order to offer the vibration of it, but once you do offer the vibration of it, it will not be long before you *are* living it.

The more often you play this *Finding-the-Feeling-Place Process,* the better you will be at playing it, and the more fun it will become. When you pretend, or selectively remember, you activate new vibrations—and your point of attraction shifts. And when your point of attraction shifts, your life will improve regarding every subject for which you have found a new *Feeling Place.*

This process works best if your range on
the Emotional Guidance Scale is within the following:

10. Frustration/Irritation/Impatience
11. Overwhelment
12. Disappointment
13. Doubt
14. Worry
15. Blame
16. Discouragement
17. Anger

Marital Situation: I still love my wife, but our relationship is nothing like it used to be. When we were first married, I couldn't wait to see her at the end of the day, and now, to be honest, I sort of dread going home. She complains a lot about so many different things, and I think she blames me for everything that isn't going the way she wants it to. I don't want to leave, but it's sure not fun staying, either. *I feel frustration. I feel blame. I feel irritation.*

The Remembering Technique: I remember the day we first met. She got my attention right away. I liked the way she looked, and I really liked how much fun she was. I remember noticing how good she was at really listening when I spoke, and how good she made me feel because she was so interested in what I had to say. I knew immediately that she was someone whom I wanted to spend more time with. . . .

(Remembering something from the past that felt good is a powerful tool for improving your vibration, because as you recall those better-feeling times, you activate the vibration that was active then. Also, it is not possible for you to focus upon what *is* happening, and what *has* happened, at the same time.)

The Imagining Technique: I'm imagining myself leaving the office and being happy about my work day being done. I visualize myself getting into my car. I'm proud of this car. It's really a beauty. I turn on the CD player, and my wife's favorite CD begins playing. I smile because I know she was driving my car yesterday and playing this music. We have this funny game going where she always leaves music in the player. Now I'm eager to get home and hang out with her. She's a lighthearted girl who always makes me feel glad to be with her. I'm a lucky guy. . . .

(Notice that there is nothing serious or heavy happening in this visualization. You are not trying to *make* anything happen. You are not trying to reform your wife, or change her. You are just making up a story for one purpose only: *to cause yourself to feel good at the same time that you are focusing upon something that is important to you.* This imagery, even though it may be complete fiction, has changed the relationship between the vibration that you have been offering lately about your wife, and the vibration of your desire about your wife. Things will now have to improve, and, at the very least, you feel good right now.)

Abundance Situation: My husband and I have both had jobs for years, and we saved some money—not a lot, but enough to live on for a year. We had a really great idea for our own business, and we had a friend who had enough money to help us get started, but now, after two years, we're still taking money from our savings to live on, and our balance is going down fast. *I feel worried. I feel discouraged.*

The Remembering Technique: I remember getting my first real paycheck and how good it felt. I had no bills, and having that much money handed to me all at once made me feel rich. I remember feeling excited that, week after week, I was going to receive another check and another. . . .

(Reactivating a good-feeling memory is an extremely helpful technique, because it is something that actually happened to *you*, so it has a factual or true nature, which holds little contradictory vibration for you. In other words, you believe it. When you reach into your past and activate a belief that matches your current desire, you are now, in that moment, in vibrational alignment—and your manifestations will now improve.)

The Imagining Technique: I'm writing the last check that will pay our friend back the money he loaned us to start our business. He's surprised and pleased that we were able to do it so quickly. I can visualize how happy my husband is as he hands our friend the check. They're such good friends. It felt good that our friend believed in our idea, and it feels wonderful that our idea paid off and we're having such wonderful success. And we're just getting started. There's so much more yet to be discovered, experienced, and enjoyed. . . .

(You cannot focus upon what you want and what you do not want at the same time. By using your imagination to deliberately conjure a good-feeling scenario, you immediately distract yourself from the unwanted reality, and your vibration shifts instantly, allowing your vibrational alignment with your own desires.)

If you really understood the power of your vibration, you would never focus upon an unwanted reality again, for your reality is extremely temporary; and it can be easily molded into situations, events, scenarios, and conditions that please you.

Planetary Situation: The planet seems unstable. There are so many earthquakes, mudslides, tidal waves, and hurricanes that suddenly sweep in and cause destruction. I almost don't want my family to leave home for fear something will happen and we'll be separated from each other, be hurt, or even worse. *I feel worried. I feel insecure. I feel fear.*

The Remembering Technique: I remember being a child, still living at home with my parents. There were two big lilac bushes in our front yard up against the fence. My mother used to let me take some old blankets outside, and I remember using clothespins to make a tent between those bushes. I spent hours there, setting it up, rearranging it, and playing with toys I had brought from my room. . . .

(You see, it is not necessary that you solve the problems of the world—or even the problems of your own life—before you can begin to feel better. Just by remembering a pleasant moment from a time gone by, you can reactivate your vibration of Well-Being, and when you are consistently *feeling* Well-Being, nothing other than Well-Being can be your experience.)

The Imagining Technique: I see myself and my wife and my kids getting out of our car at this wonderful hotel in the mountains. It's not a very well-known place, but we go there every year. The kids always look forward to coming here because they're allowed to have the run of the place. They always meet other kids, and this carefree environment just feels great to all of us. We don't try to keep any strict schedules. We just do what we feel like doing, when we feel like doing it.

(The exercise of *thinking thoughts to deliberately produce a feeling* rather than thinking a thought and then having a feeling response is an extremely valuable tool. When you care about how you feel, and you choose your thoughts because of the way they feel, you are in control of your vibrations and of the relationship between your desires and beliefs.)

Many people believe that daydreaming or fantasizing is a frivolous use of time. We see it as utilizing your <u>Emotional Guidance System</u> for the purpose of directing the power of your mind to activate the vibration, which is your point of attraction. We see it as powerful Deliberate Creating.

There is not a great difference between remembering and imagining, for in either case, the object of your attention is not actually occurring in your <u>now</u> reality. When you focus positively, apart from whatever is happening right now, you can activate a vibration that will attract something different into your experience. But if you insist on giving your attention only to the reality that exists, then nothing can change.

꧁ ꧁ ꧁ ꧂ ꧂ ꧂

Chapter 40

Applying the Becoming-Free-of-Debt Process

This process works best if your range on the Emotional Guidance Scale is within the following:

10. Frustration/Irritation/Impatience
11. Overwhelment
12. Disappointment
13. Doubt
14. Worry
15. Blame
16. Discouragement
17. Anger
18. Revenge
19. Hatred/Rage
20. Jealousy
21. Insecurity/Guilt/Unworthiness
22. Fear/Grief/Depression/Despair/Powerlessness

To begin the process of *Becoming Free of Debt,* obtain a columnar writing pad with as many columns as you have monthly expenditures. Now, beginning in the far left column, write a heading that describes your largest monthly outgo. For example, if the largest check you write each month is your house payment, then you would write as a header: House Payment. Next, on the first line beneath that header, write the dollar amount of your house payment. Now circle this amount, which represents the amount you are obligated to pay each month, and then on the third line, enter the total outstanding debt for this House Payment category.

Next, in the second column, enter your second largest payment, your third largest payment in the third column, and so on. And across the top of your columnar pad, write the following affirmation: *It is my desire to keep my promise regarding all of these financial obligations, and in some cases, I will even do twice as much as is required.*

Each time you receive a bill, get out your columnar pad and adjust, if necessary, the minimum monthly amount that is required. If it stays the same, then write the same figure.

The first time you receive a bill, or when it is time to make the payment for the category that is on the far right column of your pad (in other words, the smallest payment you make each month), write the check for exactly twice what is required. And as you do so, write in the new amount of that outstanding balance.

This may seem a little strange to you when you first begin to play the game, but even if you do not have enough money to pay everything you owe in all of the columns, still double the payment in the far right column. And feel glad that you have not only kept your new promise to yourself to do your best to pay everything you owe, but to do even twice that amount in some cases.

Because you are now looking at your finances in a way that is new, your vibration will begin to shift right away. As you feel even the slightest bit of pride for keeping your word, your vibration will shift. As you keep your promise about doubling up on some payments, your vibration will shift. And with this shift, even if it is slight, things will now begin to change in your financial condition.

If you will take the time to really enter everything you owe onto the columnar pad, your newly focused attention will begin to positively activate circumstances around the subject of money for you. Instead of feeling discouraged as you find yet another bill in your mailbox, you will feel an eagerness to enter the bill onto your columnar pad. And with this shift in attitude and vibration, things will begin to change in your financial picture.

Money that you were not expecting will appear in your experience. Bargains will reveal themselves, so your dollars will go further than you expected. All kinds of unusual financial things will occur, and when they do, be *consciously* aware that these things are happening in response to your newly focused attention and the resultant shift in your vibration.

As extra money appears, you will find yourself eager to apply another payment to the far right column. And soon, that smallest debt will be paid, and you can eliminate that column from your pad. Column after column will disappear as your financial gap between what is coming in and what is going out widens.

Your sense of financial Well-Being will improve on the first day you play this game. And if you will take the game seriously, your vibration around money will shift so significantly that you can be debt-free in a short time, if that is your desire.

There is nothing wrong with debt, but if yours feels like a heavy burden, then your vibration around money is one of resistance. When the burden has lifted, when you feel lighter and freer, your resistance has lifted, and you are now in the position to allow Well-Being to flow abundantly into your experience.

Any of the processes that help you feel better will also cause a shift in your vibration around money. However, this process is especially powerful if you are troubled about your financial situation, because it will cause you to look at your financial situation from a different perspective.

Without realizing it, day by day you will have adopted a vibrational pattern about money in response to what is happening, but you had no vibrational control when you merely had a feeling response to the situation.

This *Becoming-Free-of-Debt Process* elicits from you the same responsible approach that you are accustomed to regarding money, in that it asks you to keep records and to identify the amount of your debt, and so on, but it elicits a different perspective from you at the same time. You will immediately begin to feel a shift as you think about what you *can* do instead of what you are unable to do. It is a pragmatic approach, with a playful twist, which will shift your Energy in the direction of your desire.

If you will continue the process for a few weeks, within that short period of time your dread and fear that you may have developed around the subject of money will be replaced with hope, fun, and eagerness. This game will lead you out of debt, if that is your desire; it will help you to, once and for all, balance your Energy around the subject of money, and it is our promise to you: Once you balance your Energy regarding money, your total financial balance will come into alignment as well. But without the balancing of Energies, there can be no financial balance.

࿔ ࿔ ࿔ ࿔ ࿔ ࿔

Chapter 41

Applying the
Turning-It-Over-to-the-Manager
Process

Imagine that you are the owner of a very large corporation and there are thousands of people who work for you. There are employees who assist in the manufacturing and marketing of your products; there are bookkeepers, accountants, and advisors. There are artists, advertising experts—thousands of people, all working to make your company successful.

Now, imagine that you do not personally work with any of these people, but you have a manager who does; and your manager understands them, advises them, and directs them. So whenever you get an idea about something, you express it to your manager, who says, "I'll take care of that right away." And he does. Efficiently. Effectively. Precisely. Just the way you like it.

You may be saying to yourself right now, "I'd love to have a manager like that—someone I can count on, someone who would work on my behalf."

And we say to you, *You __do__ have a manager who is that and much more. You have a manager who works continually on your behalf called the __Law of Attraction__, and you have only to ask in order for this Universal Manager to jump to your request.*

The key to the success of this process is to make requests with an *expectation* of the request being fulfilled. It's like asking someone you trust, who has never let you down, to do something, knowing full well that he will get it done. That is the attitude from which you must make your requests to the Universe. *Make your requests with the attitude of expecting results.*

This process works best if your range on the Emotional Guidance Scale is within the following:

10. Frustration/Irritation/Impatience
11. Overwhelment
12. Disappointment
13. Doubt
14. Worry
15. Blame
16. Discouragement
17. Anger

Neighbors' Situation: I used to like this neighborhood, but then some people moved in next door and they're just awful neighbors. Their dog uses our yard for a bathroom, and they have three or four junker cars parked in their driveway instead of on the street in front of the house. I'm embarrassed to have people over to visit. *I feel blame. I discouraged. I feel anger.*

But now, I remember that I have this capable, effective, willing Universal Manager who works expressly for me. So I ask for the following, doing my best to remember that this manager is really, really good, and will be able to effectively satisfy my requests:

I would like this dog to find another place, away from my yard.
I would like these junker cars to be moved from this street.
I would like to have a good relationship with my neighbors.
I want to be proud to live on this street.
Thank you for taking care of these things.

Home-Maintenance Situation: Our house is costing us a fortune just to keep things working. It wasn't built very well to begin with, and now it's ten years old and things are constantly breaking down. Every time I turn around, something else needs to be repaired. *I feel frustrated. I feel overwhelmed. I feel disappointed. I feel discouraged.*

But now, I remember that I have this capable, effective, willing Universal Manager who works expressly for me. So I ask for the following, doing my best to remember that this manager is really, really good, and will be able to effectively satisfy my requests:

Please find a reasonably priced, talented, versatile repairman.

I would like him to determine which things should be replaced.

Please locate those items at very good prices.

I want to realize the many advantages of this mature property.

I want the past disadvantages of this older property to be eliminated.

That's all for now. Thanks for taking care of these things.

Adult-Child Situation: I have an adult daughter who's always mad at me. No matter how much time I spend with her, it's never enough. When I *am* with her, she spends most of our time complaining about how we don't spend enough time together! I'm so busy, and I don't have much time to spend with her, but it's really not fun to be with her because of the way she feels. *I feel guilty. I feel angry. I feel disappointed.*

But now, I remember that I have this capable, effective, willing Universal Manager who works expressly for me. So I ask for the following, doing my best to remember that this manager is really, really good, and will be able to effectively satisfy my requests:

Amplify my daughter's best qualities to me.

Amplify my best qualities to my daughter.

Remind each of us, many times a day, about what good lives we are living.

Orchestrate a really wonderful outing for us to spend together.

Take care of some of these details that I have been spending so much time on.

That's all for now. Thanks for taking care of these things.

Abundance Situation: My husband and I have both had jobs for years, and we saved some money—not a lot, but enough to live on for a year. We had a really great idea for our own business, and we had a friend who had enough money to help us get started, but now, after two years, we're still taking money from our savings to live on, and our balance is going down fast. *I feel worried. I feel discouraged.*

But now, I remember that I have this capable, effective, willing Universal Manager who works expressly for me. So I ask for the following, doing my best to remember that this manager is really, really good, and will be able to effectively satisfy my requests:

Please line up a strong, steady flow of customers for us.

Inspire a buzz around the area about our business.

Inspire us to perform any appropriate action.

Help our friend feel our genuine appreciation for his help.

Bring us the staff we will need to operate this expanding business.

That's all for now. Thanks for taking care of these things.

Loneliness Situation: I don't have many friends. I don't even have one really close friend, and it's not much fun going through life alone. I've had friendships in the past, but nothing that really clicked. It seems like people are just looking for what they can get out of me, but then they don't really want to give anything back to me. *I feel discouraged. I feel lonely.*

But now, I remember that I have this capable, effective, willing Universal Manager who works expressly for me. So I ask for the following, doing my best to remember that this manager is really, really good, and will be able to effectively satisfy my requests:

Please set up some circumstances where I can meet some nice people.

Arrange people who are a match to me to rendezvous with me.

I would like them to be interesting, fun, and self-sufficient.

I prefer meeting people in a way that feels completely natural and unforced.

I would like this to begin happening right away.

That's all for now. Thanks for taking care of these things.

Meddling-Parent Situation: I haven't lived at home for over ten years, but my mother still thinks that she needs to tell me what to do, so I avoid her because I don't like being bossed around. And then she gets mad, and that's even worse. But when we're together, she treats me like I don't know how to live my own life. *I feel blame. I feel anger.*

But now, I remember that I have this capable, effective, willing Universal Manager who works expressly for me. So I ask for the following, doing my best to remember that this manager is really, really good, and will be able to effectively satisfy my requests:

Please remind my mother than I'm now grown up.

Please point out to my mother how very capable I am.

Please lovingly soothe any of my mother's discomfort.

Guide my mother to other meaningful things she can turn her attention toward.

Help my mother know how much I love her.

Organize our times together so that we're both feeling great.

That's all for now. Thanks for taking care of these things.

Acting-Career Situation: I've wanted to be an actress since I was a little girl. I took some classes and found out that I'm pretty good at it. I get acting work from time to time, but nothing exciting, and nothing that I really want. It's hard. There are so many people applying for the same work that I am that it seems hopeless. Maybe I should just forget about it and go get a real job. *I feel disappointed. I feel discouraged.*

But now, I remember that I have this capable, effective, willing Universal Manager who works expressly for me. So I ask for the following, doing my best to remember that this manager is really, really good, and will be able to effectively satisfy my requests:

Arrange some great auditions for me.

Get the word out there that I am available and that I am good.

Put my résumé on the top of the pile for consideration.

Line up any trainers who would enhance my evolving talent.

That's all for now. Thanks for taking care of these things.

Financial-Imbalance Situation: I can't get ahead. It seems like things constantly come up, so I have to spend everything I make. And I have a lot of credit card debt, too, so I'm really spending more than I'm making. I try to budget, but everything just costs so much. My wife works, and that helps. But as our kids get older, things cost more for them. *I feel worried. I feel discouraged.*

But now, I remember that I have this capable, effective, willing Universal Manager who works expressly for me. So I ask for the following, doing my best to remember that this manager is really, really good, and will be able to effectively satisfy my requests:

Arrange for an increase in my wages.

Arrange for an increase in my wife's wages.

Find lower-interest credit cards for us.

Remind me frequently what a great life I'm living.

Instill appreciation in me and my wife for the wonderful things we have.

Guide us, in some way, to the best financial decisions from where we are now.

That's all for now. Thanks for taking care of these things.

Financial-Security Situation: My husband and I have both worked our entire lives. We've always been very careful with our money, because we knew that at some point we would want to retire. We managed to accumulate a very nice nest egg. Our son, who works as a stockbroker, said we should let him invest it, and that we could really increase our savings for our retirement. So we gave him the money to manage, and now it's all gone—everything that we've worked for our whole lives. I don't see how we'll ever be able to retire. *I feel worried. I feel discouraged. I feel blame. I feel anger. I feel insecurity. I feel fear.*

But now, I remember that I have this capable, effective, willing Universal Manager who works expressly for me. So I ask for the following, doing my best to remember that this manager is really, really good, and will be able to effectively satisfy my requests:

Help us regain our feeling of prosperity.

Find a faster way of accumulating value from our existing resources.

Point out any current advantages that we may have been missing.

Let our son know that we aren't holding any grudges.

Inspire a "fresh start" attitude in us.

That's all for now. Thanks for taking care of these things.

Travel Situation: I feel so limited. I seem to be able to explore or understand only a tiny part of this world. There are so many places I'd like to visit, but I can't get enough time off from work to go very far, or to stay long enough to really discover anything. I feel like I'm missing out on so much. *I feel bored. I feel disappointed.*

But now, I remember that I have this capable, effective, willing Universal Manager who works expressly for me. So I ask for the following, doing my best to remember that this manager is really, really good, and will be able to effectively satisfy my requests:

Clear a spot in my itinerary for an exploratory vacation.

Line up a satisfying route that will satisfy many of my interests on this first trip.

See what you can do about getting especially good prices on everything involved.

Bring the information to me as you find it, even though the trip is still off a ways.

Arrange the financing for this and future trips.

That's all for now. Thanks for taking care of these things.

Environmental Situation: I'm afraid that we're destroying our planet. The air isn't clean anymore. You can't drink the water; it's poison. Fish are dying; the ice caps are melting. *I feel blame. I feel anger. I feel insecurity. I feel fear.*

But now, I remember that I have this capable, effective, willing Universal Manager who works expressly for me. So I ask for the following, doing my best to remember that this manager is really, really good, and will be able to effectively satisfy my requests:

Make sure the planetary utilities are performing properly (that is, earth in orbit, water movement around the planet, gravitational pull. . . .)

Restore our water to its former purity.

Orchestrate appropriate weather for the earth's Well-Being.

Show me evidence of earth's Well-Being whenever you can.

That's all for now. Thanks for taking care of these things.

Government Situation: I'm very tired of the inefficiency of governmental bureaucracy. There are so many government requirements that you have to hire people whom you shouldn't even need . . . just to fill out the bureaucratic forms. You can't even get the bureaucracy on the phone to personally answer a question. I've wasted so much of my time just trying to find out what I'm supposed to do so that I can do it the way they want it the first time. We need a better bureaucratic system. *I feel frustration. I feel overwhelmed. I feel blame.*

But now, I remember that I have this capable, effective, willing Universal Manager who works expressly for me. So I ask for the following, doing my best to remember that this manager is really, really good, and will be able to effectively satisfy my requests:

Line up effective employees for government offices.

Help our government create user-friendly guidelines and forms.

Bring people to me who understand the requirements.

Find a way for us to find easy compliance with these requirements.

Remind me often of the things that are in my greatest interest, that I should give attention to.

That's all for now. Thanks for taking care of these things.

Government's Financial-Deficit Situation: Our government is so inefficient and ineffective. If it needs more money, it just arbitrarily takes it from us. There's no financial accountability; money is spent so foolishly, and then they complain that there isn't enough for the things that really matter to *us.* What a mess. I don't know how anyone could ever straighten it out. *I feel disappointment. I feel blame. I feel anger.*

But now, I remember that I have this capable, effective, willing Universal Manager who works expressly for me. So I ask for the following, doing my best to remember that this manager is really, really good, and will be able to effectively satisfy my requests:

Guide people in government to fiscal responsibility.

Make arrangements so that we get more for every tax dollar spent.

Show me evidence of progress regarding government value and efficiency.

Put leaders in place who are focused on making things better.

I want to see less partisanship and more sincere interest in issues.

That's all for now. Thanks for taking care of these things.

National-Pride Situation: When I was a kid, I felt so passionate about my country. I was thrilled when I heard patriotic songs, and I loved to hear stories of things that had happened as our nation was forming and we were evolving. But I don't feel patriotic anymore; I guess I know too much now. I don't feel good about decisions my government is making. *I feel disappointment. I feel blame. I feel anger.*

But now, I remember that I have this capable, effective, willing Universal Manager who works expressly for me. So I ask for the following, doing my best to remember that this manager is really, really good, and will be able to effectively satisfy my requests:

Inspire the next generation of leaders and get them ready.

Amplify the intentions of the citizens of this nation so that leaders can hear them.

Put leaders in place who are responsive to the desires of those they serve.

Show me things that inspire my pride in my nation.

Line up compelling information for our leaders to consider.

Remind our leaders that they are responsible to us.

That's all for now. Thanks for taking care of these things.

When you first play this game, you may find yourself challenging your own requests by doubting that your wishes will be carried out by your Manager. And, of course, if your doubt is more dominant than your desire, you will be right, and you will see no evidence of your intentions being satisfied.

If you will continue to play the game, getting into the spirit of delegating to this Universal Manager, your doubts will fade, your expectations will increase, and you will get evidence that will confirm the power of your *own mind. <u>It is an exciting day when you come into conscious awareness of the amazing power of your intentions.</u>*

We cannot begin to describe to you the resources that you have at your fingertips—those that defy description are standing in readiness to assist you. You have only to find a way to access those resources, and the *Turning-It-Over-to-the-Manager Process* is just the tool to help you to do that. Over time, this process will change your perception of your life—and when your perception of your life changes, your life will change.

❧ ❧ ❧ ☙ ☙ ☙

Chapter 42

Applying the Reclaiming-One's-Natural-State-of-Health Process

D o this process while lying in a comfortable place—the more comfortable, the better. Choose a time when you have approximately 15 minutes when you are not likely to be disturbed by anyone.

This process works best if your range on the Emotional Guidance Scale is within the following:

10. Frustration/Irritation/Impatience
11. Overwhelment
12. Disappointment
13. Doubt
14. Worry
15. Blame
16. Discouragement
17. Anger
18. Revenge
19. Hatred/Rage
20. Jealousy
21. Insecurity/Guilt/Unworthiness
22. Fear/Grief/Depression/Despair/Powerlessness

Now, write the following short list in a place where it will be easy for you to read, and then, when you first lie down, read it slowly to yourself.

- *It is natural for my body to be well.*

- *Even if I don't know what to do in order to get better, my body does.*

- *I have trillions of cells, with individual Consciousness, and they know how to achieve their individual balance.*

- *When this condition began, I didn't know what I know now.*

- *If I'd known then what I know now, this condition couldn't have gotten started.*

- *I don't need to understand the cause of this illness.*

- *I don't need to explain how it is that I'm experiencing this illness.*

- *I have only to gently, eventually, release this illness.*

- *It doesn't matter that it got started, because it's reversing its course right now.*

- *It's natural that it would take some time for my body to begin to align to my improved thoughts of Well-Being.*

- *There's no hurry about any of this.*

- *My body knows what to do.*

- *Well-Being is natural to me.*

- *My Inner Being is intricately aware of my physical body.*

- *My cells are asking for what they need in order to thrive, and Source Energy is answering those requests.*

- *I'm in very good hands.*

- *I will relax now, to allow communication between my body and my Source.*

- *My only work is to relax and breathe.*

- *I can do that.*

- *I can do that easily. . . .*

Now, just lie there and enjoy the comfort of your resting place, and focus upon your breathing—in and out, in and out. . . . Breathe deeply while still remaining comfortable. Do not force it. Do not try to make anything happen; there is nothing for you to do other than to relax and breathe.

You will very likely begin to feel soft, gentle sensations in your body. Smile, and acknowledge that this is Source Energy specifically answering your cellular request. You are now feeling the healing process. Do nothing to try to help it or intensify it. Just relax and breathe—and allow it.

If you were experiencing pain when you laid down, follow the same process. However, if you were feeling pain, it would be helpful for you to add these words to your written and spoken list:

- *This sensation of pain is an indicator that Source is responding to my cellular request for Energy.*

- *This sensation of pain is a wonderful indicator that help is on the way.*

- *I will relax into this sensation of pain because I understand that it's indicating improvement.*

Now, if you can, drift off to sleep. Smile in your knowledge that All-Is-Well. Breathe and relax—and trust.

Physical-Decline Situation: I worry that my body is deteriorating. I don't have the energy that I once had, and I can't do the things I used to enjoy doing. I have aches and pains, my knees hurt when I walk, and I don't dare try to run anymore. I'm scared that it's going to get worse and worse. *I feel worried.*

My body is flesh and bone, but my body is also vibration.

The way my body looks and feels is a result of my vibration.

My body is as it is right now, and that is all right.

My body is continually changing, and that is all right.

My vibrational offering affects the changes in my body.

Physical decline is about vibration, not about passing through time.

It is possible for me to pass through time and improve my vibration.

Physical decline is neither natural nor necessary.

I do not have to wait for others to know this or demonstrate this.

I can begin now, or whenever I choose, to demonstrate this.

A shift in my vibration won't give me instant physical evidence.

A shift in my vibration will give me instant emotional evidence.

Once I achieve a vibrational shift and stabilize there, I'll see evidence.

I'm willing to shift my vibration and wait for the physical evidence.

Feeling better emotionally will be adequate evidence for now.

Finding and maintaining positive expectancy is wonderful.

I can feel my body benefiting from my newfound ease.

I can feel the stability of my physical body.

I can feel the life-giving qualities of my new Energy alignment.

I can feel that I'm coming into Energy Balance.

I can feel how much my body enjoys my Energy Balance.

All is well with me right now—and getting better still. . . .

If you will take the time to deliberately improve your *emotional* feeling about your physical body, your *physical* conditions will improve. Lead your improved conditions with improved expectations and watch what happens. Remember, the manifestation always follows the vibration, and 99.99 percent of every creation is already complete before there is any physical evidence.

Focus upon your Emotional Journey and find improvement there; and the physical, Action Journey must follow. It is law! There are no exceptions to this!

Chapter 43

Applying the Moving-Up-the-Emotional-Guidance-Scale Process

Here is the way we would apply this powerful process: When you are aware that you are feeling some rather strong negative emotion, try to identify what that (feeling) emotion is. In other words, consciously think about whatever is bothering you until you can pinpoint the emotions that you are experiencing.

This *Moving-Up-the-Emotional-Guidance-Scale Process* can be used no matter what your emotional state of being, but it is particularly helpful when you are feeling particularly bad.

Considering the two extreme ends of this *Emotional Guidance Scale*, you could ask yourself, *Do I feel powerful, or do I feel powerless?* While you may not actually be feeling either one of these emotions precisely, you will be able to tell which way your emotional state of being is leaning right now. So, in this example, if your answer is *powerless,* then shorten the range that you are considering. In other words, ask yourself, *Does this feel more like powerlessness or frustration?* Still more like powerlessness. Then shorten the range still further: *Does this feel more like powerlessness or worry?* As you continue (there is no right or wrong approach to this), eventually you will be able to state with accuracy what you are really feeling about the situation you are addressing.

Once you have found your place on the *Emotional Guidance Scale,* your work is to try to find thoughts that give you a slight feeling of relief from the uncomfortable emotion you are feeling. A process of talking out loud or writing down your thoughts will give you the best reading of the way you are feeling. As you make statements with the deliberate intention of inducing an emotion that gives you a slight feeling of relief, you will begin to release resistance, and then you will be able to move gradually up the vibrational scale to a place of feeling much better. Remember, an improved feeling means a releasing of resistance, and a releasing of resistance means a greater state of *allowing* what you really want.

So, using the *Emotional Guidance Scale,* and beginning with where you are, look at the emotion that is just about where you believe you are now, and try to fashion some words that will lead you into a slightly less resistant emotional state of being.

A Scale of Your Emotions
Would Look Like This:

1. Joy/Knowledge/Empowerment/Freedom/Love/Appreciation
2. Passion
3. Enthusiasm/Eagerness/Happiness
4. Positive Expectation/Belief
5. Optimism
6. Hopefulness
7. Contentment
8. Boredom
9. Pessimism
10. Frustration/Irritation/Impatience
11. Overwhelment
12. Disappointment
13. Doubt
14. Worry
15. Blame
16. Discouragement
17. Anger

18. Revenge
19. Hatred/Rage
20. Jealousy
21. Insecurity/Guilt/Unworthiness
22. Fear/Grief/Depression/Despair/Powerlessness

Remember, you do not have access to emotions that are far from where you are currently vibrating. Therefore, although you may have spent an entire day beating the drum of the emotion where you are, on the next day, try to establish a different set-point even if it is only a slight improvement.

If the negative emotion you are feeling is slight, you will quickly move up the *Emotional Guidance Scale.* If the negative emotion you are feeling has begun only recently, you will quickly move up the *Emotional Guidance Scale.* If you are experiencing something extremely serious, or it is something that you have been troubled with for many years, it is conceivable that you could spend as many as 22 days moving up this *Emotional Guidance Scale,* each day deliberately choosing the improved emotion just above the one you are currently feeling. But 22 days from *Powerlessness* to *Empowerment* is not a long time at all when you compare it to people you know who have been in a state of grief, insecurity, or powerlessness for many years.

Now that you understand that your goal is to simply reach a better-feeling emotion, it is our expectation that this process will free you from troubling negative emotions that you have been experiencing for years. And as you gently and gradually release the resistance you have unknowingly gathered, you will begin to experience gradual improvements in your life experiences . . . in all troubling areas of your life.

Meddling-Parent Situation: I haven't lived at home for over ten years, but my mother still thinks that she needs to tell me what to do, so I avoid her because I don't like being bossed around. And then she gets mad, and that's even worse. But when we're together, she treats me like I don't know how to live my own life. *I feel blame. I feel anger.*

No matter what I do, my mother is never happy with me. (powerless)

I don't want to see her, but I feel guilty when I don't. (guilt)

My mother has always been disappointed in me. (unworthiness)

Nothing I do pleases her. She finds fault with everything I do. (unworthiness)

I hate spending time with her. (hate)

After being with her, it takes days to recover. (hate)

I'd like to go far, far away from her where I would never see her. (revenge)

I wonder what she'd think if I just vanished. (revenge)

Maybe then she'd miss me, or remember something good about me. (revenge)

She'd probably be glad I'm gone. (anger)

She'd have to find someone else to pick on. (anger)

I don't really plan on going anywhere. But I'd like to. (discouragement)

I wish I could think of a way to get away from here and from her. (discouragement)

I shouldn't have to be looking for a way to escape. (blame)

Your mother should uplift you, not make you want to escape. (blame)

I wish she could have been different. (disappointment)

My friends' mothers are very different from mine. (disappointment)

There are so many things, on so many levels, wrong with our relationship. (overwhelment)

I wouldn't know where to begin to sort this out. (overwhelment)

Ten years of therapy hasn't helped at all. (overwhelment)

She makes absolutely no effort. (frustration)

She thinks our problems are really all my problems. (frustration)

She thinks she's always right and I'm always wrong. (frustration)

She is just that way, and I don't believe she will ever change. (pessimism)

She can't see my point of view at all. (pessimism)

I don't think she even tries to see it from my point of view. (pessimism)

I should just accept that that's how she is. (contentment)

It's not my job to change her. (contentment)

I'm not the only one who finds her difficult. (contentment)

Maybe, when we're both much, much older, we'll get along better. (hopefulness)

Maybe I can reach the place where what she thinks doesn't matter so much. (hopefulness)

Maybe in time, she'll understand my point of view. (hopefulness)

Maybe, in time, I'll understand her point of view. (hopefulness)

Maybe, in time, neither of us will be bothered by the other. (hopefulness)

I really want to love my mother. (hopefulness)

I want my mother to love me. (hopefulness)

I know that she does love me on some level. (hopefulness)

I know that she thinks she's helping me. (hopefulness)

She means well, misguided as she is. (optimism)

I should just let this go. (optimism)

It would feel so great to just let this go. (eagerness)

I'd love to not be bothered by this any longer. (eagerness)

My life is so good, in nearly every area. (enthusiasm)

I've managed to do pretty darn well in most areas of my life. (enthusiasm)

I have a great life, when I take the time to notice. (enthusiasm)

I love feeling good. That's who I really am. (happiness)

I know I'm supposed to feel good. (empowerment)

I know I'm supposed to feel good, and I want that on all levels of my being. (empowerment)

I have the ability to feel good, no matter what. (empowerment)

It's not my mother's job to make me feel good. (empowerment)

I can't change my mother's opinion about anything. (empowerment)

I can control my opinion about everything, even my mother. (empowerment)

My mother birthed me into this wonderful body and life experience. (appreciation)

Bless her heart. I've given her a run for her money. (love)

I love my life. I'm so glad to be here. (appreciation)

I know I'm good. I know I have value. I do know that. (knowledge)

All is well with me. (knowledge)

I feel so very good. (joy)

I have so much that I want to do. (joy, passion, eagerness)

Financial-Security Situation: My husband and I have both worked our entire lives. We've always been very careful with our money, because we knew that at some point we would want to retire. We managed to accumulate a very nice nest egg. Our son, who works as a stockbroker, said we should let him invest it, and that we could really increase our savings for our retirement. So we gave him the money to manage, and now it's all gone—everything that we've worked for our whole lives. I don't see how we'll ever be able to retire. *I feel worried. I feel discouraged. I feel blame. I feel anger. I feel insecurity. I feel fear.*

Our savings are gone, and we have no way to gather them again. (fear)

It took our whole lives to save it and only days to lose it all. (grief)

We don't have enough time left to accumulate what we need for retirement. (insecurity)

It's not right that some get richer while those like us lose everything. (hatred)

I hope the market really crashes and they lose everything, too. (revenge)

It's outrageous that so many people were negatively affected. (anger)

There should be some reasonable protection against things like this. (discouragement)

We should not have trusted the people who were advising our son. (blame)

They're in the business. They should have been more cautious. (blame)

They're only interested in their commission. (blame)

They don't really care about their clients. (blame)

I hope our son realizes who he's working with before it's too late. (worry)

There's no way to protect yourself against things like this.
(doubt)

We were so looking forward to a comfortable retirement.
(disappointment)

We have so much to do, and so little time to do it, in order to be ready. (overwhelment)

We should not be in this predicament at our age. (irritation)

No one is adequately addressing this issue. (frustration)

I guess most people just give up and take whatever comes.
(pessimism)

We are, however, in better shape than many people.
(contentment)

Our home is paid for, and it's a nice place to live.
(contentment)

Nothing should prevent us from continuing to live here as long as we like. (contentment)

We both like being active. (contentment)

There are many possibilities that we haven't even considered yet. (hopefulness)

Our financial picture did gain quick momentum for a while before it bottomed out. (optimism)

It's possible that something could come up that would be very helpful. (optimism)

While I can't see a viable avenue right now, something could surprise us. (optimism)

We've had to dig in before, and when we get determined, things do happen for us. (positive expectation)

We're far from finished. (positive expectation)

Although we've lost our savings, we haven't lost our experience. (belief)

We're stronger and clearer as a result of this experience. (positive expectation)

It will be fun to see what the future brings. (enthusiasm)

I think we'll surprise ourselves by how productive we can be. (eagerness)

This has been interesting, to say the least, and we do feel more determined and more alive than before. (eagerness)

I feel a new determination bubbling within me. (empowerment)

I look forward to what the future holds. (passion)

I know that everything will be all right. (knowledge)

Things always have a way of working themselves out. (knowledge)

We've always been incredibly blessed. (appreciation)

Strife-and-Starvation Situation: Our whole world is such a mess. There are so many wars, so much conflict, and so many people suffering. I don't understand why, when we have all this technology and so many resources, there are so many people who are still going hungry. It seems like we should have figured things out better by now. *I feel discouraged. I feel blame. I feel anger.*

We have the technology to feed the world. Why aren't we doing it? (anger)

I would donate some of my extra money, but I don't believe those who need it will get it. (discouragement)

Those in roles of authority should do their jobs more effectively. (blame)

There are so many people who are suffering. (worry)

The pattern is so pervasive, and I see no improvement coming. (doubt)

We, as a civilization, should have come along further by now. (disappointment)

There are so many in need, but we're so disorganized. (overwhelment)

We need to get organized. (frustration)

I don't believe anyone really cares. (pessimism)

I'm tired of thinking about it. (boredom)

Surely there are people out there with good ideas. (hopefulness)

Every improvement springs forth from someone's idea. (optimism)

Even this nation hasn't always thrived, but for the most part, we are now. (optimism)

Just as our lives in this nation have steadily improved, it can be that way for others, too. (positive expectation)

I want people all over the world to thrive and be happy. (eagerness)

I want to travel and to experience, firsthand, this amazing world. (enthusiasm)

I want to show myself that Well-Being does dominate this planet. (eagerness)

I want to be an example of one who thrives. (eagerness)

I love my nation and the life that I'm living. (appreciation)

I love understanding that I can control my life by deliberately offering thought. (freedom/empowerment/joy)

I love knowing that we each have the ability to create the lives that we choose. (knowledge)

Environmental Situation: I'm afraid that we're destroying our planet. The air isn't clean anymore. You can't drink the water; it's poison. Fish are dying; the ice caps are melting. *I feel blame. I feel anger. I feel insecurity. I feel fear.*

I don't want to contribute to the destruction of our planet, but I'm only one person, and my actions have such little effect. (powerlessness)

What if, in our ignorance or greed, we've created a lifestyle that really is destroying our planet? (fear)

If studies are proving that our emissions really are harmful, how could any rational politician continue to allow that harmful action to continue? (rage)

Politicians should be held responsible for their irresponsible acts. (revenge)

Instead of being rewarded for their bad judgment, they should be punished. (revenge)

They have access to the facts, yet they continue in the same direction. How do they sleep at night? (anger)

They're all the same. (discouragement)

Our leaders are corrupt, and our voters are complacent. (blame)

We're moving in a very dangerous direction. (worry)

I see no signs of things improving. (doubt)

When I was younger, I thought our leaders were wise, wise people. (disappointment)

So much needs to be changed. (overwhelment)

Everyone understands that we need change, but no one steps up to do anything about it. (frustration)

Everyone seems to be happy as long as they're getting theirs. (pessimism)

I'm weary of the whole discussion. (boredom)

I may as well mind my own business and focus on my own life, which is going well for the most part. (contentment)

Maybe things will improve, or maybe they aren't as bad as I think they are. (hopefulness)

This is a very large planet, and it's been around for a very long time. There's definitely a pattern of stability. (optimism)

Our behavioral patterns are continually molded by our exposure to experience, and it will always be that way. (positive expectation)

I'm so looking forward to discovering for myself, firsthand, the beauty of this planet. (eagerness)

I'm making a list of extraordinary places that I intend to visit. (eagerness)

This is a wonderful time to live—one in which we can travel and explore so easily. (appreciation)

If I really wanted to, I could buy a airline ticket today, and travel anyplace I really want to go. (freedom)

We live in a wonderful time. (joy/knowledge)

Citizens'-Freedom Situation: It feels as if our personal freedoms are rapidly eroding. Our government seems to have gone crazy in using its strong-armed tactics under the guise of serving the "greater good." What about *my good?* What about the good of those like me? They've gone crazy. I know this wasn't what our Founding Fathers had in mind. They're probably rolling over in their graves. *I feel disappointment. I feel blame. I feel anger. I feel insecurity. I feel grief. I feel powerless.*

How in the world did we ever get to the place where these people in government are in power? (powerlessness)

I can't imagine what possible rationale they have for their ridiculous actions. (powerlessness)

I don't understand why there isn't a tremendous public outcry. (despair)

It's truly frightening when people who clearly lack the ability to see the big picture have power. (insecurity)

How is it possible that anyone could be so blind or inconsiderate about the lives of humans around the world? (rage)

How can they do what they do and live with themselves? (rage)

I hope they wake up one day, fully aware of the damage they're causing? (revenge)

I wish they could experience suffering in their own lives. (revenge)

When someone is informed and tries to make a difference, they're eliminated. (anger)

No one is willing or capable of stepping up and doing what's right. (discouragement)

The attitude of corruption permeates and saturates our political system. (blame)

We don't see who they are until it's too late. (worry)

They're not true to their word. (disappointment)

It's a tangled mess that seems impossible to unravel. (overwhelment)

Where's the public outcry? (frustration)

People are uninformed or complacent, or they just don't care. (pessimism)

However, I'm not personally impacted by them in any great way. (contentment)

History has shown us that when things really get bad, the tide always turns eventually. (hopefulness)

There must be brilliant people all over the world who are gathering clarity from the experiences we're having together. (optimism)

Great leaders are born from difficult situations. (positive expectation)

Young people all over the world are gaining clarity and strength. (positive expectation)

Future generations always become purer and clearer as a result of those who've gone before. (positive expectation)

When you look at it from a broad view, life on this planet is getting better and better. (positive expectation)

As billions watch, observe, and formulate their own personal preferences, a worldwide asking does occur. (eagerness)

Source answers our individual and collective asking, and that process supersedes the pettiness of politics. (empowerment)

No one has any power in my personal experience. (empowerment)

I am, and we all are, the creators of our own experience. (empowerment)

Through focus, I can feel as good or as bad as I choose to feel. (empowerment)

Through my choices, I offer vibrations that equal my own personal point of attraction. (empowerment)

It's the same for everyone. (empowerment)

Chapter 44

The Value of Utilizing These Processes

The most important thing that we want you to derive from reading through the processes we have just offered is a clear understanding of what your real work as a Deliberate Creator is: to bring the Energy of *your* Being, into alignment.

In every example offered here, and in the examples from your own life, when you feel negative emotion it always means the same thing: You have a desire pulsing within you that you are resisting and preventing from being actualized because you also have a contradictory vibration that is active. These processes have been offered to illustrate how to reduce that contradictory vibration.

It is likely, as you read through the processes, that you found yourself arguing with us, on one topic or another, that the process or solution we offered did not solve the problem. *I can't see how this process is going to stop the ice caps from melting . . . or actually make my neighbor get rid of the junk cars in front of his house. . . .*

But do not lose sight of what your work really is: the balancing of Energy between your most often active vibrations (beliefs) and your desires (intent). You must not put yourself in the impossible position of needing your neighbor to get rid of the junk cars before you come into Energy alignment. Your happiness cannot depend upon what your government does or what your mother does, or whether the ice caps are melting or not. You must get control of the vibrational relationship between your desires and your beliefs if you are going to be a Deliberate Creator and be effective in accomplishing your own goals and desires, or be living in joy.

Do not underestimate the power of Energy Alignment. The masters of your societies, the creative geniuses of your past and present civilizations, found this alignment . . . There is a substantial difference in the words "believe in your dreams" and actually being in vibrational alignment with your dreams. Your words are not your point of attraction—but your vibration is.

If you will deliberately apply these processes, with the intention of bringing the vibrations of your Being into alignment, these processes will render you powerful—and in doing so you will become the powerful, joyful Deliberate Creator of your own experience.

Chapter 45

Ninety-Nine Percent of Every Creation Is Complete Before You See Any Evidence of It

You are now aware that you are the attractor or creator of your own experience, and we want you to realize that only you are the attractor or creator of your experience. We believe that you now understand, more clearly than ever before, how it is that you create, for you now realize that you are continually broadcasting a vibrational signal, which is your point of attraction.

It is our desire that you are also now aware of your *Emotional Guidance System,* which indicates the vibrational relationship between your focused thought, in this moment, and the vibration of your desire. You can literally feel when you are moving toward or away from something wanted, and you can also feel when you are moving toward or away from something unwanted.

We are pleased that you now understand, or at least are beginning to understand, that you can make every journey—from where you are to where you desire to be—quantifiable. Your journey to success on literally every subject of your desire need never again be confusing or confounding, for clear emotional signals are there to guide you in the direction of anything and everything you desire.

Your day, every day, is comprised of stimulating, interesting, thought-provoking moments that cause you, whether you know you are doing it or not, to emit vibrational signals that are projected into your future, and they are responsible for everything that happens to you.

Every circumstance, every event, and every meeting of every person— everything that you live—is because of what you have been thinking about, wondering about, pondering, remembering, observing, considering, and imagining. . . . You are literally thinking your life into being.

We are extremely pleased that you now understand the importance of your conscious awareness of your emotions, for they help you to understand—as you are remembering, pondering, observing, or imagining—whether you are preparing your future with something you will enjoy when it manifests, or something you will not enjoy. And since 99 percent of every creation is complete before you see any physical evidence of it, it is extremely valuable to understand what your emotions are telling you about the direction of your thoughts right now.

By utilizing your *Emotional Guidance System,* you are able to direct your thoughts in the direction of pleasing things *before* they manifest. But if you wait until a manifestation has occurred before you begin to redirect your thoughts, it is a much more difficult process for you, because once some unwanted thing has manifested, it is now much harder to focus upon what you desire.

When you accept that you are, right now, in the process of creating things that will manifest into your experience, and you are <u>deliberately</u> guiding your thoughts to good-feeling ideas . . . your future manifested experience will be filled with things that will delight you as they unfold into your experience.

This book has been written to assist you in your conscious awareness of the unseen things (for now, anyway) that you are in the process of creating. We do not believe that you would deliberately choose to bring cancer, a car accident, a financial disaster, or a divorce into your experience, but because so much thought about those things is often offered without your conscious awareness that you are doing it, you are often surprised when an unwanted thing occurs. It sometimes seems to have come out of nowhere. But it did not come out of nowhere, and it did not come instantly. It came, finally, after many, many thoughts that had matched it radiated from you.

But now, after reading this book, you will no longer be surprised when things, good or bad, manifest. For you will never again focus a thought and feel the corresponding emotion that indicates whether you are moving toward, or away from, something you want without knowing it. The vibrational relationship between your *now* and your *future* creation is now known by you.

The end of the *Emotional Guidance Scale* that feels like passion, joy, appreciation, and love feels the way it does because of your perception of your own personal empowerment and freedom. The other end of the *Emotional Guidance Scale* that feels like depression and fear feels the way it does because of your own personal perception of disempowerment and bondage. But now, disempowerment need never be your experience again, for you know too much at this point.

You now understand that the only thing that could ever prevent you from the joyous abundance of all good things you desire is your own vibrational offering that takes you in the opposite direction of those things.

You now understand that your glorious emotions are helping you establish your route or course, on all subjects, and that by following the trail of increasingly good-feeling emotions, you will project vibrational rockets into your future, which will yield a steady stream of lovely creations.

Now, when you feel frustration mounting, or impatience or anger surfacing, you can stop in a moment of true realization and ponder: *Just what am I projecting into my vibrational escrow? Should I take a moment now and redirect my thoughts and change the course of my probable manifestation, or should I just let my thoughts run away with me—supported by Law of Attraction—and just live the consequences of my unmanaged, undirected thoughts?*

And although you can turn anything around at any time, even after manifestation, it is our encouragement that you turn it around while it is being vibrationally formed—for it is ever so much easier then. But even more important, we want you to consider the millions and millions of moments of your real-life experience that could be feeling good *now,* feeling good *now,* feeling good *now.*

Yes, of course, the manifestation will come. It certainly will come, good or bad. Wanted or unwanted, it is coming. But your life is *now,* your emotions are *now,* and the way you feel is *now.*

Direct your thoughts to improve your *now* moment—and the manifestations will take care of themselves.

We very much enjoy seeing your lives unfold, from our Non-Physical vantage point . . . If you could see your future as we see it, you would realize that there are things wanted and unwanted that are, at this very moment, taking shape and form right outside your door. And today, tomorrow, and the next day, you are going to add one more thought, one more focused vibration, to what is already there, which will cause the tipping point, or manifestation point, for you. So it is really worth tuning in to your glorious *Emotional Guidance System* to be aware of what you are on the brink of manifesting.

You come forth into this body, focused in this Leading-Edge time-space reality, because you adore creation. There is nothing in all of the Universe that is more satisfying to you than to mold the Energy that creates worlds with the power of your own focused mind.

You did not come forth to fix a broken world, for your world is not broken.

You did not come forth to help others see the error of their ways and redirect them.

You did not come forth to gain the approval of another through some specific course of action.

You came forth into this magnificent contrast for the thrill of feeling your own personal preferences being born. You came forth, understanding that you would then be able to feel the vibrational relationship between your new desire and your current perspective, and you looked forward to the process of balancing the Energy of those two vibrational vantage points.

You came forth for the joy of giving birth to new desire and for the thrill of the balancing of Energy process.

And yes, you looked forward to the manifestation of your creations, but your true emphasis has always been upon the 99 percent of the creation that happens *prior* to manifestation. *The thrill of the manifestation, no matter what the creation, is but a brief thrill that quickly becomes the platform from which you launch your next and your next and your next creation. But your life, from your physical vantage point, or from your Non-Physical vantage point, is really about the 99 percent of creation that happens before manifestation.*

Today, no matter where I am going, no matter what I am doing, no matter whom I am doing it with . . . nothing is more important than that I feel good.

Today, I will look for that which I am wanting to see.

I am the creator of my own reality.

Right now, I will reach for the best-feeling thought that I have access to.

Thought by thought and feeling by feeling, I will focus the vibrations of my mind into alignment.

I will feel for the true vibrational essence of my Being, and I will guide my every thought into vibrational alignment, for that is the true meaning of a balancing of Energy.

᠊ᡦᡧ᠊ᡦᡧ᠊ᡦᡧ ᡦᡧ᠊ᡦᡧ᠊ᡦᡧ᠊

Chapter 46

The Amazing Power of Deliberate Intent

We have written this book in response to your asking, for you want to understand who you really are and how you fit into the larger picture. And you want to understand the purpose of this life experience and how you can best fulfill your reason for being here in this body at this time.

We want you to remember that you are an Eternal Creator who has come forth into this Leading Edge to experience the joyous expansion of your Universe. We want you to remember your value, to know your worthiness, and to love your life.

We can feel the amazing power of your intent to understand how to deliberately create your own reality, and you have literally summoned us forth to help you remember who you are and what you really know.

There is nothing more important for you, or more satisfying, than to come into deliberate alignment with your Source. To not only recognize the Energy of your Source, but to deliberately align with it, is the ultimate experience of bliss. This is the true meaning of *balancing of energy,* and it is the most important part of your life experience.

When you are in vibrational alignment with your Source, whatever you are focused on is receiving the focus of the Energy Stream that creates worlds. The power of that alignment cannot be adequately expressed in words, but you can feel it. You feel it in your joy, love, exuberance, and passion.

If you have studied with us over time, or even in the reading of this one small book, you have been introduced to a variety of games, processes, or techniques. It is not necessary for you to attempt to apply all of them, or even most of them, for they are all offered for the same reason, and each of them has power within them. *Every process, as you apply it, will raise the vibration of your Being. Every process, as you apply it, will bring you into closer alignment with who-you-really-are. Every process will give you the feeling of relief, which indicates the releasing of resistance. Every process will help you balance your Energy. Every process will help you shorten the time between where you are currently standing and where you really intend to be.*

Do not make hard work of the application of these processes. Choose one that is most appealing and use it as long as it still feels good. Then choose another and another. . . . The most important thing for you to remember is that the better you feel, in any moment in time, the more in alignment with your Source and your desires you are. And nothing is more important than that you feel good.

It is our desire that this book has liberated you from the only thing that could ever bind you or give you the impression that you are not free, for the only bondage that really exists is the *perception* of powerlessness. You are only powerless if you are not in alignment with your power, and only you possess the key to that alignment. No one can take that from you. It is only yours to hold.

So, your work, your only work (but it is your steady work, for it is work that cannot be completed) is a constant awareness of the vibrational relationship between your focus in this moment, and the focus of your Inner Being in this moment.

Your Inner Being is aware of your hopes and dreams and is focused upon them. When *you* fail to focus upon them, you feel the resistance. Your Inner Being is aware of your value and worthiness; when *you* focus otherwise, you feel the resistance. Your Inner Being expects your success; when *you* do not, you feel the resistance. Your Inner Being enjoys the continual process of expansion; when *you* are impatient, you feel the resistance. Your

Inner Being knows that you are Eternal; when *you* feel you do not have enough time, you feel the resistance. Your Inner Being knows there are no limits to your ability to create; when *you* feel diminished, you feel the resistance. Your Inner Being adores others who share your planet; when *you* find fault with them, you feel the resistance. Your Inner Being knows that everyone has access to this same power—when *you* take responsibility for the lives of others, you feel the resistance.

So pick and choose among the techniques that we have offered, and remember that there is no one right way to accomplish this alignment. Play with it, be flexible about it, try as much as you can, and do not judge your results. Just make a decision that no matter what the topic of discussion—be it from the past, present, or future—you are going to approach it in the best-feeling way that you can, from where you are right now. And with that decision, your life will turn immediately in the direction of thriving.

We have written this book to help you understand the following most important things in response to what we have been hearing from so many of you:

- You are a Vibrational Being, first and foremost, and you live in a Vibrational Universe.

- The vibrations of this Universe are perfectly managed by the powerful *Law of Attraction.*

- You cannot cease continually offering vibrations.

- The *Law of Attraction* makes it easy for you to fall into habits or patterns of vibrational offering.

- Watching people around you influences your vibrational offerings.

- Observing your own life experience influences your vibrational offering.

- Most people offer vibrations primarily in response to what they are observing.

- The vibrations that you offer are your point of attraction.

- What you think, the vibrations that you offer, and what you are living always match.

- No matter what words you use—"I'm focusing; I'm thinking; I'm remembering; I'm pondering; I'm observing; I'm imagining; I'm dreaming"—you are offering vibrations that the *Law of Attraction* is responding to.

- The more attention you give to any thought, the more dominant it becomes in your vibration.

- Your life experience is only about the thoughts you think.

- You are the creator of your own reality.

- Whenever you give your attention to anything, you activate the vibration of it in you.

- The more you give your attention to any thought, the more active it becomes in your vibration, until, in time, it becomes a dominant vibration, or a dominant player in your point of attraction.

- Those dominant vibrations are at the basis of everything you are living, and of everything you believe.

- A belief is only a thought you keep thinking.

- Through much experience, much observation, and much focusing of thought, you attract the physical manifested equivalent.

- Ninety-nine percent of every creation is completed before you see any physical evidence of manifestation.

- Right now, your future is full of potential manifestations as a result of the thoughts you have been thinking.

- Some of those manifestations will please you when they manifest, and some of them will not please you.

- It is much easier for you to turn the tide of your vibration more in the direction of things you want to experience *before* a manifestation takes place.

- There are many things that you desire, in various stages of readiness for you to experience, and your *Emotional Guidance System* will help you continue to move toward those wanted things.

- You must find a way to deactivate your vibration regarding any unwanted things that are making their way into your immediate and distant future.

- Deactivation of unwanted vibrations is the same process as activation of wanted vibrations.

- You cannot activate something wanted and something unwanted at the same time. It is one or the other—and your emotions are very clear about which way you are focused.

- It is necessary that you quantify each journey by being aware of the emotions that you feel before you can move only toward wanted outcomes.

- You are Pure, Positive, Source Energy, focused in your physical body, intending to benefit from contrast because it helps you to decide and define your unique preferences.

- By reaching for the best-feeling thoughts you can find, regarding any subject at any time, you are tending to the vibrational relationship between your now, in-the-moment thoughts, and the thoughts of your Source.

- So, as you are moving through your day today, be aware that you are creating your own reality. Feel the emotions that float upward into your conscious awareness, and acknowledge their enormous value to you.

- No matter how the emotion feels, good or bad, soft or strong, smile in recognized pride at your awareness of the emotion and of its meaning to you. Acknowledge that it is a vibrational indicator pointing out to you your alignment to your Source and your desires.

- No matter what the current emotion within you, feel glad for your awareness of it, and know that anytime, anyplace, and under any circumstance that you choose, you can choose thoughts to improve your emotion, and therefore improve the vibrational relativity between you and You.

- See yourself as Energy.

- See your Source as Energy.

- Be ever aware of the vibrational relationship between those Energies.

- The balancing of the Energy of your Being is not something like a college degree, that once you achieve it, it is yours forevermore. It is, or it is not, in the moment. You can always feel your alignment or misalignment, your balance or imbalance, your Connection or disconnection, your allowing or disallowing of that Connection.

- You are Source Energy, here in this physical body, and life is supposed to be good for you.

- You are worthy. You are blessed. You are creator. And you are here on the Leading Edge of thought to experience the joy of riding the wave of expansion that is the promise of this everlasting life.

- You cannot get it done. Not ever!

- You cannot get it wrong because it is never done.

We want to express our acknowledgment of the value of your life. It is our desire that you make peace with where you are on every subject in your life, understanding that from there you can go anywhere you choose. If you condemn your current position, or feel guilty or blame about where you stand, your future will offer little change at all. But as you soften your discomfort and try to improve the way you feel just a little bit, your vibration will begin to shift, the *Law of Attraction* will help the momentum to continue, and you can get to where you want to be in a very short period of time.

Be easy about it. Be playful about it. Every day say to yourself, *Nothing is more important than that I feel good. The better I feel, the more I am allowing all of the wonderful things of life to flow to me.*

There is great love here for you.

And for now, this book is complete.

ᥱᵹᥱᵹᥱᵹ ᧒ᥰ᧒ᥰ᧒ᥰ

Abraham Live

Questions and Answers

This is a transcript of the *Art of Allowing* workshop
(edited slightly for clarity) that was recorded
in Tampa, Florida, on Saturday, January 8, 2005.

Abraham: Good morning. We are extremely pleased that you are here. It is good to come together for the purpose of co-creating, do you agree? You are knowing what you are wanting? Are you enjoying the evolution of your own desire? Here it comes: You are thrilled with unfulfilled desires? "Oh yes, especially those, especially those."

We are so looking forward to the time . . . we can feel it in your vibration; we can see it unfolding in the ethers of that which is your future experience; we can almost hear the words flowing forth from you as you say, *I am an eternal Being,* which means: *I will never get it done,* which means: *Contrast will continue to provide new preferences within me,* which means: *Source Energy will continue to answer the preferences that are born within me,* which means: *There will always be something that I have defined as a desire that is yet not manifested—it must be that way. If I am an Eternal Being—and I am* (you say, or we are saying for you), *then there must always be unfulfilled desire.*

And we want you to become at one with that idea, because when you make peace with the idea that there will always be something that you want and you have not yet figured out *how* it will come, *when* it will come, *where* it will come from, or *who* will assist it in coming—when you get comfortable with that never-ending, ever-unfolding of that which is your life experience, then you will begin to live as you intended as you came forth: joyously expanding, never complete.

Sometimes we hear you speak of the word *perfect,* and perfect sounds sometimes (or feels in the vibration that you offer when you say it) like you think that you will get everything checked off your list, and then life will be *perfect.* "Once I'm looking at all conditions that please me, then life will be *perfect."* And we say, then you would be dead. And we do not mean dead the way you mean *dead;* we mean dead in the way that there is no dead. We mean finished. We mean opposite of the Eternal Being that you are.

So when you get it, that you are Eternal and that (even in this focused body, in this magnificent, Leading-Edge, time-space reality) as experiences cause new desires to be born within you, if you can relax and understand that that is the way that it must be and enjoy the fact that it is not all done, and look forward to the unfolding of it, then you are in this place where you are balanced right on this Leading Edge, and it is like riding the crest of a wave.

So when we talk about Balancing of Energy, when we talk about coming into alignment with who you are, when we talk about being a vibrational match to who-you-really-are, when we talk about your desires and your beliefs matching—what we are really talking about is using your emotions to help you contour your own vibrations into alignment. And when you do that, your circuits are wide open.

When your circuits are wide open (circuits to what? circuits to Source), *you must thrive.* You are clear-minded, you are sure-footed, you feel good, and everything in your experience is delicious. You are then the Being that you *were* before you came forth into this body, only you are more than the Being that you *were* before you came forth into this body because now you are the Being that *has* come forth into this body. Now, you are the Leading-Edge Being on the Leading-Edge experience, tuned in, tapped in, turned on to the Source Energy from which you come, which is expanding right along with you. (Is it not good?)

We want to assist you in recognizing—more accurately, and earlier—when you are in vibrational alignment with what you want. We will show you how you can, with so little effort (so much less effort than it takes to learn a computer program), become in vibrational awareness of what your vibration is. And then what you do about it is certainly up to you.

This *Art of Allowing*—we love those words. *Art of Allowing* is what we are calling this gathering—allowing my Connection to my Source; that is really what that means. It does not mean the art of putting up with, or tolerating, all kinds of awful things. It means: *the art of finding my alignment, and therefore, living in joy no matter what's happening around me. It means: achieving such vibrational alignment with who I am by looking for positive aspects and by making books of appreciation, and by wanting so much to feel good—that I hold myself consistently in vibrational alignment with who-I-really-am.* And then, even though contrast is going to be in my experience, and even though there may be problems that I project into my future, as fast as I project any problem (which is really the *asking,* is it not?) right on its heels will come the answer.

You can get so good at projecting problems or questions into your future—with answers right on the heels—that the answers can actually manifest simultaneously with the problem so that the problem never even reaches your awareness. That is creation at its best, where the contrast keeps producing the new, better experience, and before you even have a chance to notice that you are missing the new, better experience, and that it has not come about—it comes about.

To live with questions, and as quickly as you can identify that you want to know or that you need to know, or that you would like to experience—circumstances and events have already been arranged so that you are living what you are wanting almost as fast, or even *as* fast, as you are asking about it.

It is a lifelong art. You will never get it done. You will come back lifetime after lifetime for the joy of it, not because there are some rungs on a ladder that you must climb, not because you are getting marks on the chart, not because there is some hierarchy that you are hoping to achieve, and not because you are wanting to achieve some sort of perfection and then never come back again. You are creators who love creating! And we are here to tell you that there is no place anywhere, anytime, anyplace, that is more delicious than this time-space reality in which you are focused. The contrast is so prevalent. The variety is so amazing. Your ability to focus has never been better. And now you are remembering who you are and coming back into alignment so that you will be the absolute enjoyers of the joyous life that you are creating.

We are eager to talk with you about anything that is important to you. There is nothing off limits here. You will notice a wonderful unfolding, as the question that was perfect to lay the basis for your question will have preceded it. Everything that you are about is known by us. Do not worry; we will not reveal anything that you do not want to be revealed. We are sensitive to your privacy issues.

It is important that you explain the nitty-gritty of your experience, to a certain extent, so that others listening in can notice the vibratory match of where you are and your vibration. But we will not get too carried away in that. For it is our desire to assist you in Balancing your Energies relative to anything that is important to you. We want you to align to the things that you have desired. We want you to understand that every experience that you have lived—the good ones and the ones that you call "not so good" . . . have launched desires into your future experience that are being held for you . . . *for you!*

They are encoded by your vibration—they are yours. They are being held for you in vibrational escrow. And when you bring yourself into vibrational alignment with those things that you have let the Universe know you want (and you know, you have been letting the Universe know, incrementally, different aspects of your desire), the Universe has coupled all of those different aspects of all of your different desires into the perfect unfolding. *There are things that you have not even thought of that are in your future because they are the combination of the desires that you have already launched out there.*

Someone coined a very wonderful phrase when they said, "Be careful what you wish for because you may get it." And we say, *whatever you think about is in the vibrational offing for you. It is just a matter of how much in alignment you come with it.*

Good. You have some things you want to talk about? Yes? Some things.

Minister Discovers Jesus' Teachings in Abraham

Guest: I want to thank you and Jerry and Esther for what you're doing, because it's very powerful stuff, particularly this latest book. *(Ask and It Is Given)* I'm a minister [at a local church], and we're using your material, have been for some time. I have a question on *beliefs*. From what I've read, and from what I understand from my own Being, beliefs are nothing but solidified old thoughts used over and over again until they become operational in you.

Abraham: Thoughts you keep thinking. A thought that you activated so often that it became a dominant activated thought. Yes.

Guest: It also seems to me that you can't change those beliefs, but you can just create a new one and operate on the new one. In other words, if I start operating from joy, and I, maybe, used to operate from rage, I can operate from joy most of the time, but that rage seems to still be there. Once in a while I slip, catch myself, and move back.

Abraham: Well, here is how it works. Every thought that you ever thought still exists. But every thought that you ever thought is not, right now, activated within you. It is like there are radio towers transmitting all kinds of signals all around you. Radio signals, television signals, cell-phone signals, all kinds of signals are flowing through here right now. But you do not necessarily know those signals are here unless you turn on a receiver that receives one of them. It is your vibration that activates your receiver, which then makes you involved with whatever signals you have activated.

You said something very good that we want to qualify just a little bit. You said you cannot necessarily change a thought or a belief, but you can choose a different one. And that is accurate. But we would like to say, you might activate that thought pretty regularly, and the *Law of Attraction* will help you make it easy to keep activating that thought. But if you are wise enough to know that that activated thought does not feel very good, then you might choose a thought that feels *slightly* better than that. Now, if you choose a thought that feels *really* better than that, the *Law of Attraction* does not help you find it because your signals are too far apart. But if you choose a thought that feels slightly better, and you deliberately activate that, then what happens is that the newly activated thought becomes your Vibrational Set-point, or belief, and this other one sort of diminishes. In time, it may not come again at all. As you are consciously reaching for the better and better and better-feeling thought, what happens is, you sort of deactivate those other unwanted thoughts.

Now, we want to be clear about this. You cannot really deactivate a thought; that is what you are saying. You cannot deactivate that thought, but you can activate that other thought. And the more often you activate that other thought, then the easier that thought, and other thoughts like that thought, come to you.

So, let us say you have done that. You have worked. You feel, on the whole, better and better and better. Then something happens that has not happened in a while, and you see it on television, and it causes you to focus, and it causes you to activate a thought that has not been activated in a long while. Well, do not panic. Just understand that something happened that activated a thought, and if you will reach for a thought that feels a little better, you can move yourself into another place.

And, in fact, that is what *bridging beliefs* really is. One subject at a time, you just reach for a better-feeling thought, reach for a better-feeling thought . . . Let us say that there are a hundred different subjects that you activate often that are, sort of, negative activations, but one at a time, you make yourself feel better. So now, you have about 50 of them that feel pretty good, and 50 of them that do not feel so good. But, one at a time, 49 and 48 and 47, you reach for a better-feeling thought. And in time you have 90 things that mostly you feel good about, and only a few things, like maybe taxes or the government bombing people or tsunamis . . . big things that really do not have so much to do with you personally on a day-to-day basis, but they bother you when you look at them. And, one at a time, you make a decision and line up with it, and make a decision and line up with it. Until, before you know it, you are in alignment, because you have made the *Emotional Journey,* which is easy, as opposed to the *Action Journey,* which is impossible in many cases. Now you have brought yourself consistently into alignment with feeling good.

So then a question is: "Could I reach the place where I've trained myself into feeling so good that nothing would ever happen that would make me feel bad again?" And we say, who cares? You have the ability to make *that* feel good, too. In other words, maybe once you get a hundred cleaned up, there are a hundred more that are less severe that you want to clean up. And maybe after you get those cleaned up, there are a hundred more that are even less severe that you want to get cleaned up. And maybe, after you get up here in *hope* . . . and *optimism,* you may want to move them all into *appreciation, joy,* and *ecstasy.*

There is no end to your journey. You will never reach the place where you want to isolate yourself from the contrasting experience that causes you to focus. What you are looking for (ah, and thank you for helping us say it) is creative control of your own focus. We do not want your government to have to stop doing what it is doing so that you can feel good. We want you to train yourself to feel good, no matter what. We do not want people to treat you nicely and not hurt your feelings so that you can feel good; we want your feelings to be unhurtable. *We want you to be so aware that you can change the way you feel—just by wanting to and by focusing—that you are now no longer fearful about what is going on out there in the world.*

You are not afraid of dying; you are in love with living. You are not worried about people doing things that displease you. You are in creative control of your vibration, and therefore, you are in creative control of everything that happens to you.

Guest: So it's just a process.

Abraham: It is a never-ending, joyful process. That is why, if you are in one of these lower vibrations where it feels like *fear, anger,* or *rage,* do not beat up on yourself. Say, "Ah, my blessed *Guidance System* is letting me know that I have some old stuff activated. And it does not matter. It's not my mother's fault. It's not the government's fault. It's a process of what I've lived. *The bottom line is, I don't like the way I feel. So I need to look someplace else, or I need to make peace with that as it is. But I need to adjust the way I feel."* And you have the power to do that.

When you show yourself that you have the power to do that, then, and only then, are you really free. Because no one can bestow this freedom upon you—freedom is bestowed. In other words, it is the basis of this Universe. You are so free that you can choose bondage. You *are* free. But the only way you will ever perceive that freedom is by understanding that you have the ability to feel good, no matter what.

And when you reach that place where fear is gone, you are in that place of freedom. Now you can go anywhere. Now you can have a wonderful time, no matter what, you see. Yes.

Guest: Thank you very much. There's a group of scholars called the "Jesus Seminar" who have isolated what they believe Jesus really said. And it condenses down to a few pages. And when I read just that, what they say, it is obvious that he was teaching exactly what you're teaching.

Abraham: Same Energy.

Guest: Absolutely.

Abraham: Jerry has a friend who speaks mostly just Spanish, and Jerry wanted to convey to him his love and appreciation. So Jerry wrote a long letter in English and took it to another friend who speaks Spanish, and had it translated into Spanish. He gave the letter to his friend, who was most appreciative. Then, a few weeks later, Jerry had the letter still with him and met another person who was a translator of English and Spanish. So he had the same letter translated now from Spanish back into English. And when he read the letter, he hardly recognized it.

Guest: That's exactly what happened.

Abraham: Jerry said, "This is just one letter that went to one person and then to one other." Can you imagine? These two translators had no intentions other than to do their best to convey the message, and with no ulterior motives that they were trying to direct or guide or anything. And so it's no wonder that those scholars have whittled the teachings down to just a few words. Most of them have been enormously distorted or omitted to serve the purpose of whoever was, in the moment, doing the redeciphering.

And that is why we do not think it is a good idea for you to count on Esther's translation, either. We think you should get your own.

Cat Lover Has Problems with Refrigerated Animals

Guest: Hello, Abraham. Thank you for your patience with us.

Abraham: It is easy to be patient when you know all is well.

Guest: Do souls, human and animal, travel together lifetime after lifetime?

Abraham: Yes.

Guest: How do I contact those in the Non-Physical realm, including my cats?

Abraham: You want to meet up with them in the Non-Physical? You said "lifetime to lifetime," which made it sound like physical lifetime to physical lifetime. So, you are wanting to meet up with your cats in the Non-Physical, or just in future physical lifetimes?

Guest: Both.

Abraham: Well, the nice thing about that is that you do not have to orchestrate that from your physical perspective. And that is good, because it is a big order of business, and most of you do not believe that you can. So, the only two things that are required for the achievement of anything is to set forth a desire and then to allow it to be. When you come forth into your future physical experiences, especially as little ones, you rendezvous, as children, with lots of familiar pets from other experiences. It is only as an adult that you begin to question whether you can do that or not.

Have you not known lots of beasts that reminded you of lots of other beasts? You see? And humans have a hard time with this next thing that we are going to say, but sometimes one of your very familiar-feeling animal friends is actually a part of the same Energy Stream that you are. Humans worry about that because you are so happy by being at the top of the food chain, or the "karmic wheel," that you do not really want to share it with beasts in that way. In other words, "Bring me my pet and I will love him, but I do not want to be on the same Vibrational Non-Physical wavelength that is him."

We want you to know that Energy is Energy, and that you come here to your physical experience with different *intentions*, but it is the same Non-Physical Energy Stream. And the essence of that which is in the animal is not so very different from the essence of that which is in the human. It is all Pure, Positive Energy.

The only difference worth mentioning between human and beast is that the beast, without exception, is more tuned in, tapped in, turned on. They are more in touch with who they really are. Part of the reason is that they do not hide behind language. Part of the reason is because they have shorter life experiences and they do not have as much opportunity to build up as much resistance. In other words, when you hear about the butterfly or the bird that is migrating long distances and you say, "Well, who knew? Who was leading the crew? Who knew where to take them?" we say, Broader Perspective. They were tapped in to Broader Perspective.

Have you ever watched a flock of birds and watched them fly, and wondered why they are not banging into each other? They were not practicing when you are not looking. In other words, they get into that zone where their Broader Perspective knows every part of the formation. And they fulfill their role, because they instinctively (is one way of saying it), but they intuitively (is another way of saying it), but they vibrationally, "aligningly" know how they fit into things, you see. And you all are working on figuring that out, too.

Have you ever been driving where you could just feel yourself in the flow of traffic, and you look up ahead and you have a sense of what is going to happen? And you slow before you even see the taillights on the cars ahead of you? Or you change lanes even before there is a reason, a visual reason, for you to change lanes. . . . You're doing the same thing that your beasts are doing. You are operating from a Broader Perspective.

Guest: Okay. This kind of leads to the next question. I struggle with *allowing* family and friends who eat animals (due to the suffering of the animals) especially when co-habiting with someone who desires to have dead animals in the refrigerator and cook them in my house. Can you help me with this?

Abraham: Not really.

Guest: It's a tough one.

Abraham: Well, you have set yourself up for a lot of grief because you keep beating the drum. You used every word that you could use to make that a bad thing. So, here is what we would say to you. You cannot have it both ways. You cannot vehemently disapprove of that and have dead carcasses in your refrigerator at the same time. In other words, something must give—and we would work on getting in the flow with the nature of things.

In other words, it is possible that some ruler could become so powerful and get such a big bomb that he could convince all other humans never to eat animals. But you are not ever going to convince the other animals not to eat other animals. The big one is always going to eat the little one. In other words, the big fish is always going to eat the little fish. And when you get into the rhythm of that, when you understand that the animals coming forth come forth knowing that, then you do not make it such a big deal.

And we promise you that, as clear-minded as these beasts are (all of you, coming in), if it was not a game they wanted to play, they would not come forth again and again to play it with you, you see. You can let that one go. You do not have to eat meat—but do not push against something that is so prevalent in your society that you have to cringe at it.

A friend was talking about not wanting to drop bombs on people. And Esther told Jerry the other day that if he reads one more bumper sticker and gets upset about it, she is going to make him ride in the bedroom of the motor coach with the windows closed. Because he sees bumper stickers that he does not agree with, and then gets all stirred up about it. And Esther wants to put blinders on him so that he does not get upset.

The world is full of people who have opinions that are different from yours. And you just have to finally make up your mind that you are not the only one with an opinion. *Everybody gets to have opinions, and everybody gets to put bumper stickers on their car, and everybody gets to live and feel as they want to feel. It is your job to find your way of feeling good within it; it is not their job to make bumper stickers that please you.*

To Soothe Mate After Frightening Diagnosis

Guest: What can I do to help my husband? He's just gotten a very serious diagnosis, and he's very, very fearful.

Abraham: Well, how are *you* doing? Are you fearful, too?

Guest: Well, I'm trying not to think about it, but I have pains in my stomach.

Abraham: When you *do* think about it, do you feel fear?

Guest: Yes.

Abraham: So you are not in a position to help him because you are as fearful as he is. So if you talk about it, you will just bang around there together in that fearful place. The first thing you have to do is to practice feeling hopeful until you are sure that you are more hopeful than fearful. And then you will be of great advantage to him.

Guest: Okay.

Abraham: Talk to us about whatever it is that is making you feel fearful. So, "My husband has been diagnosed with something scary." [yes] "And I'm scared." Or, "My husband has been diagnosed with something scary, and I'm feeling all right about it." Now, do you think that it is wrong for you to feel good about something that scares everybody else? This is a big question: Do you have the right, first of all, to feel good under bad conditions? [yes] Well, that is the first big step. Because if you believe that you have the right, then the next question is (setting your husband and his diagnosis aside completely), would you rather feel good or bad? [good]

Abraham: Do you think that it is possible to focus upon something that usually makes you feel bad, and feel good? [no] Well, it *is* actually possible. And that is the work you have to do. In other words, you could change the subject and just focus on other things that make you feel good, but that would not change the way you feel about this thing that makes you feel scared. So the work is, "I've got to focus upon something that, right now, makes me feel afraid, and coax myself into being able to not feel so afraid of it." That is the work. That is the *Emotional Journey.* "I've got to feel less afraid."

Guest: And how do you do that?

Abraham: Well, you do it by wanting it enough to keep trying. Let us try here. So, are you still having that fearful feeling? [yeah] Well, let us see if we can coax that out. You will know that you have done it if you start feeling relief.

Now, you are really going to like this; this is so important: Your assignment, right now with us, is to take an *Emotional Journey,* which means that your assignment, right here with us, is to change your vibration, which changes everything. It changes your power of influence, and you can help your husband once you change the power of influence. So your work right now is to take an *Emotional Journey,* which means that your work is to change your vibration, which means that your work is to feel better, which means that your work is to find relief. That is your assignment right now. Your assignment is *not* to try to find a cure. Your assignment is *not* to try to find a path that will bring this about. Your assignment is so much more simple than that: *Your assignment is to move from fear to ease.*

So with that simple assignment, just ramble. Try to detach yourself enough from the diagnosis, from the prognosis, from whatever your husband is feeling—try to detach yourself from it enough so that you can focus upon the subject and feel good while you do it, right here and now.

Guest: Okay. He's had this diagnosis, but deep inside, I don't believe it. It doesn't seem to me as if he's really ill. It almost seems to me as if this is the modern medical fairy tale kind of thing.

You know, you go to a doctor and he finds you sick. And deep inside, somehow, he looks good, to me. He doesn't have a feeling of illness, to me.

Abraham: Well, you are right there. As you said that, that feels to us like your more stable feeling. In other words, the fear that was amplified by the recent diagnosis and by your husband's response to it was a sort of blip on your radar. But what you said to us just now feels like your truer Set-point, does it not? We can feel that you feel that.

So, when we say, *Are you afraid?* your answer is: "Well, I can make myself afraid if I focus upon it in fearful ways and really listen, in the way that the doctor is pinpointing it. But I have to work harder at feeling afraid than I do about the way I really feel." Would you say that's accurate?

Guest: That's true.

Abraham: Then you are in a very good place of helping your husband. Can you hear yourself conveying that to him? When you convey that to him, does he go along with you and your stable, secure feeling, or does he argue for the limitation of the sickness?

Guest: He argues for the limitation of the sickness.

Abraham: So the doctor has more credibility with him than you do.

Guest: Always.

Abraham: So now you are in a position where you are worried about what he is doing with his vibration, because you know that what he is doing is going to affect his experience.

Guest: Exactly.

Abraham: So the *Emotional Journey* that you are taking is not about going from fear to security about the illness, because you are already secure. Your *Emotional Journey* is going from worrying about what your husband is doing in creating his own reality, to *not* worrying about what your husband is doing in creating his own reality. Does that make sense? [yes]

In other words, the *Emotional Journey* that you need to take here is about feeling secure in your husband's ability to manage his own life experience, or to come around to his own wellness. So, do you believe that he can? What is your *Emotional Set-point* on that?

Guest: Not really. I mean, I don't really believe that he can.

Abraham: You want to. You would like to hope, but . . . your belief is in a place of disbelief. In other words, you do not believe that he can, but you need to believe that he can before you can feel good, yes?

Guest: Yes, yes.

Abraham: So that is the journey that we want to take with you right now. In this little bit of time, here in this focused Energy, try to move yourself to that. Try to move yourself from *not* believing that he can clean up his vibration and do it, to believing or hoping that he *can* clean up his vibration. Make that effort. Do not lose sight of what you are doing: You just want to give *yourself* relief. You are not trying to fix him; you are not trying to make him well. You are trying to take an *Emotional Journey* where *you* feel better.

The feeling is, you are not optimistic about *his* getting hold of this, and you want to be optimistic, so what you want to do is, talk yourself into feeling more optimistic about him getting hold of this. Has he been an abject failure at everything he has tried?

Guest: Oh no.

Abraham: Oh, so he does accomplish some things. Like what?

Guest: Oh, yeah. Oh, he's been successful in business . . .

Abraham: You mean he can focus and make things happen?

Guest: Oh yeah.

Abraham: And the world responds to him in a positive way?

Guest: Very.

Abraham: So, you do not see him as someone who is incapable of making up his mind and getting what he wants?

Guest: Not at all. But on this subject, he is a little tenuous because he has an expert giving him bad information.

Abraham: Exactly. So, have you ever seen him look out into a marketplace, or look at something that did not look the way he wanted it to be, and have you ever seen him just use his will and make things turn out even though there was evidence that was to the contrary? Have you ever seen him do that? [yeah] For example?

Guest: There can be something, say, a product that shows up, and I look at it, and I say, "It's not really working well." And he says, "No, it's fine. Let go of your doubts; it's fine."

Abraham: So he *does* understand this. He understands the idea of mind over matter. He understands the idea of using his focused, sort of, willpower in order to bring things about. You have seen him have that success in his experience, yes?

Guest: Yes, but not in health things.

Abraham: Now, you just lost sight of what your goal was. Because we were leaning there; we were almost there, and then you snatched back and got something that made you feel worse. Now why would you do that? You get the sense of what we are talking about? [I do.] In other words, that is the work. You do not want to reach back and get that stuff that makes you feel worse. You want to reach out and find that stuff that makes you feel better, and you want to practice that better-feeling stuff until you can say with confidence, "My husband is a focuser. And sure, this has got him sort of knocked off of his balance a little bit; it would anybody. But I have seen him regaining his balance" relative to what? Where have you seen him regaining his balance? Have you ever seen him off his balance and then get it back? [yeah] For example?

Guest: Oh, he's a golfer. He can look outside and say, "Well, it looks like rain, but I'll go anyway 'cause it'll probably be okay. You know, it'll probably clear, and it probably will work out."

Abraham: This really is his nature, is it not? [yeah] Are you not beginning to feel foolish about your doubt in him? In other words, he is not going to have any trouble getting ahold of this once he relaxes with the idea of it a little bit. In other words, his resources are going to return, and he is going to regain his balance, like he always does. And he is going to apply himself successfully. And he has the benefit of having optimistic you—who is not really even worried about this diagnosis—tenderly coaching him toward positive expectation. Now, you feel better, do you not?

Guest: I do.

Abraham: The first *Emotional Journey* we tried to drag you along on, you did not even need; you were already there. And in the second *Emotional Journey,* you came very quickly, in a very short time, you see. So, as you find doubts creeping in, and they might, just drown them out with things that feel better, until you stand in that confident place. You are going to be bowled over by your power of influence when you are steadily in that place of *expecting* your husband to manage his life. He has been managing it so far, and doing extremely well. And there is no reason for him to stop now over some pesky thing that really has more to do with what the doctor thinks than it does to do with what *he* thinks. Yes.

Guest: Thank you.

Preschool Genius "Won't Listen to His Teacher"

Guest: My questions pertain to my five-year old son. He won't listen to me.

Abraham: Good.

Guest: He won't listen to any women. Men, a little better. A teacher asked me, "Can you get him to listen to me?" I tell her that he won't listen to *me*. And—

Abraham: Who *is* he listening to?

Guest: I guess his own head, because he told me,"You know, I live my life my way, and you do things sort of your way."

Abraham: He must be listening to *us*. (Fun)

Guest: Yes. And then he'll say, "Well, you said Abraham said . . ." He said, "I want to have fun." So the teacher said to him, "Well, do you not listen to me, Joseph, because you don't understand, or because you don't want to?" He said, "I don't want to." So she called me again. She said, well, he put a hole in his school paper. He wanted to do it, so he did it. And I said, "Joseph, you can't do that. You can vibrate what you want when you get in *your* house, but you're in mine now, so you've got to vibrate with me." So it's just the back and forth . . . it's the listening part. And then my mother pipes in with, "You should spank him; you should do this; you should do that. It didn't kill me; it didn't kill you," you know.

Abraham: Well, here is the thing. As Joseph is doing pretty much what he wants to do, if he could maintain that, then, when we visit with him 15 or 20 years from now and he is experiencing not only outrageous success in all areas of his life, but he is one of the most joyful people we have ever met, and we say, "Joseph, what is your secret?" He would say, "I had a driving influence, coming forth from within, that I listened to, louder than everybody else put together. Oh, my mother tried, yes, she did try. She even threatened to throw me out of the house. But I did not let anything dissuade me from my own *Guidance System*."

Now, we are playing with you a little bit, but it is mothers like you who have left you as the "walking wounded" that you are. In other words, so many of you are not trusting your own guidance because you have yielded to the guidance of so many others who are ill equipped to really guide you, you see. And when you think about it, that teacher is guiding Joseph so that she will get from him what *she* wants, and you are guiding him so that you will get what *you* want. And *who* gets to guide him so that he will get what *he* wants? And that is the point that he is trying to make with everyone, you see. And we do not want to hurt everybody's feelings—but we are on his side.

Guest: What about his age? I mean, isn't he kind of young . . . I just don't want him to be an adult who doesn't listen to anyone, and then . . .

Abraham: Well then, our purposes are crossed, because we want him to be an adult who does not listen to anyone. We want *all* of you to be adults who are not so controverted by what everybody else thinks that you contradict your own vibration and disallow what *you* really want.

We know what you are getting at, and here is what we would do: Here you have this little one who is rather clear about who he is, still remembering, and who is throwing some of what you are trying to teach him back at you, and who is giving you some grief here and there by not conforming. So, as you think about him and the *Action Journey* that he is taking, you have a lot of options here. In other words, you can watch it and be upset about it, or you can watch it and get into alignment with it. So tell us some of the positive aspects that you feel about him being, sort of, self-directed. Is there any advantage at all in that?

Guest: Yes, he has his own mind. And he's not a conformist. (Neither was I, when I was his age.) He tells you just how he feels so you know where he's coming from. He's not a phony person. [yes?] I think, in some ways, it will help him.

Abraham: But, beyond that, can you feel, from what you have heard today, that there is tremendous value in making up your mind and not wavering? [yes] And so, do you really want him to be someone who makes up his mind and does not waver—unless somebody else who is bigger and stronger and has more influence can get in his face and *make* him change his mind? In other words, do you want to teach him disempowerment or self-empowerment?

Guest: I want him to be self-empowered.

Abraham: And so, the only time that it conflicts with you is when *his* self-empowerment disagrees with *your* idea of what he should do?

Guest: When the teacher calls me. I just don't want to be a parent who's standing in the office because my son won't do what they want.

Abraham: But can you have it both ways? And this is the thing that we really want to put out to you: Can you have a child who is self-empowered, who really knows who he is, and a child who kowtows to what everybody else wants at the same time? [no] And how do you help him define *who* he should listen to and *who* he should not? In other words, do you want everyone who stands in the role of teacher to be someone who gets his undivided attention? Because if that is the case, then do you not want to scrutinize the teachers? Do you not want to find out what *they are* trying to motivate him to? Do you not want to find out who they are and what their real intent is? In other words, would you not like to know if they are influencing him to vote Democrat or Republican or toward being a Christian, or toward . . . ? You would like to know what their inner motivation is, would you not? And it might be really hard for *you* to sort all of that out, yes?

Would you not rather just say, "Ah, Joseph, you are someone who knows your own mind, who is tuned in to Pure, Positive Energy. I trust that you are going to be able to sort this out. And I am going to leave you to your relationships with all of these people. I am not going to get in the way and try to side with them. Or, I am not going to even get in the way and try to side with you. I am going to give you the opportunity that all of us had when we were born, of sifting through your experience, letting your experience help you define what you want—and then listening to your own Guidance to get you toward what you want."

Do you think your son would choose failure? Do you think he would choose being unkind? You never see that, do you? Do you think he would choose being lazy? You do not see that either. In other words, you have seen no evidence of anything other than brilliance in this child, yet you are afraid to let him guide himself. And we think it is because, for a long time, adults have believed that they are the wise ones who know the ways of this world, and that if they do not guide their children, their kids then will go astray. And we want you to understand how backwards that thinking is.

These are genius creators who have just arrived from the Non-Physical, who are feeling empowered, and if they would be left to their own devices, they would not go astray. They would maintain worthiness; they would maintain their feeling of autonomy; they would maintain their feeling of Well-Being. They would thrive— unless it was taught otherwise to them. In other words, if others do not do something to change their vibration, they are in a vibration of thriving. And you see evidence of that, do you not? That is what he came forth to remind you. Do you not see evidence mostly of thriving and feeling good?

Jerry and Esther had the good fortune of meeting someone who founded a school (the Sudbury Valley School in Massachusetts), and the premise of the school is that no one learns anything, really, unless they have a sincere desire to learn it. They do not teach just for the sake of teaching. If you want to learn something and you express your desire to them, they will do everything they can to assist you in learning. But no one, no teacher, no faculty member, is even allowed, much less encouraged, to go to little Joseph and say, "Wouldn't you like to read this?" or "Wouldn't you like to learn about this?" It is all left to the desire of the child.

And the reason that Jerry and Esther are so excited about it is because it is the basis of what Abraham teaches: *Unless you are asking, there is no answering that comes forth. And when you are asking, the answer is always coming forth.*

Joseph is trying to help you and his teachers remember, first of all, that he gets to choose, and that whatever he chooses will come to him. He is not worried about not toeing the line and ending up in a place of not knowing anything. You might be, and his teacher might be, but he is not worried about that. He is still in that place of remembering that if he wants it, the Universe is going to deliver it. And he frankly cannot figure out what all of the fuss is about. Is that not what he keeps saying to you over and over again? [yep] "Why are you making a big deal out of this? I'm all right. I'm doing all right." You see?

It would be like meeting someone who was born clear-minded and healthy, but that person is born into a community where most everybody limps, for whatever reason. And then their making fun of the way *he* walks because he is not yet limping. And him saying, "Hey, I know you're all limping and seem to be liking it, but I don't feel like limping and don't seem to need to." And they all say, "Limping is what we do here. Learn to limp!" And he says, "I don't feel like limping." So they just club him in the knee. (Fun!) And then he limps along. And then they all say, "Good. Good, Joseph." We are not exaggerating that! That is a perfect, perfect analogy, you see.

What he is saying to all of you is, "I don't feel like limping." Do not worry about him, and do not worry about what the teachers think about him.

Now, you have an *Emotional Journey* to take, though, correct? Because, think about it, he is who he is. And do you remember how much trouble *you* got into? You were just like him, and your mother went to a lot of trouble to try to make you different. Did it work? It just brought *you* grief and *her* grief, but it did not change your stubbornness, did it? So, you are not really eager to do that with Joseph.

So what choice do you have as you see him as this independent, genius creator that he is? Do you think that you could humiliate him into conformity? No, and you would not want to. Do you think you could punish him into conformity? That did not work with you. So what are your choices? Do you think that you can, in terms of an *Action Journey,* make him be different than he was born to be? You cannot, can you?

So you have some options here. You have this little rascal who is tuned in, tapped in, and turned on. And you can look for reasons to feel good about it, or look for reasons to feel bad about it. We do not think that the *Emotional Journey* you want to take is about changing *him,* because we think, like us, that you like him pretty much as he is. We think your problem is with the school system that does not understand what you understand or what Abraham understands or what Joseph understands. So would you say that your *Emotional Journey* is about feeling better about their ignorance?

Guest: Probably.

Abraham: Is it feeling better about their ignorance? Or (oh, we are really getting somewhere here) is it about finding a way to get them to approve of you when you have a son like Joseph? (Ooooh, that is big, is it not?)

"So, here I've got this son who behaves in a nonconforming way. Brilliant, magnificent Being." Do you want him to be different from that? Would you like him to be afraid? Would you like him to kowtow? Would you like him to do what they want him to do, or do you like him being independent?

So, the *Action Journey,* in terms of how Joseph *is,* is that you *do not* want to change, but how you *feel* about how they feel about Joseph is what you *do* want to change. So you have some choices: They are probably going to continue to disapprove of him—and you cannot make him behave in an approving way. So your choice is, they can disapprove of him and you can be all right with it, or they can disapprove of him and you can not be all right with it. Which would feel better to you?

Guest: Be all right with it.

Abraham: So now, offer some words toward that end: "I want to find a way to be all right, even when they're not all right, with how Joseph is." Ramble a little bit, and see if you can find some relief in that.

Guest: I don't want to hear them say anything to me when I walk in the door.

Abraham: All right, that is making it worse.

Guest: I just want to pick him up from school and leave, so I don't have to see them.

Abraham: Not helping.

Guest: I want to stay active in the school, like I've been doing.

Abraham: "I like my role in school. I'd like to be able to influence them a little bit. I'd like them to understand the creative geniuses that they've got. I'd like them to understand that school is not jail; school's an environment where creativity can be expressed, and it should be able to be expressed in lots of different ways. And I would like to be able to help foster the creativity—not the conformity—in these kids. And born to me is a magnificently creative child who is lighting a fire within me to want to do that, and this could be fun." That felt better. You did not say it, but it felt better when you heard it. In other words, *make yourself feel better.*

What is the goal? To feel better about how they feel about Joseph, who will not change. In other words, have you given up on the *Action Journey?* You had better, because you cannot change him. So, he is going to be like he is, and you can like it; or he can be like he is, and you can not like it. And which do you think is better for you, and which do you think is better for him?

Do you know that the magnificent genius creators of your world—every one of them without exception—were like Joseph when they were born and just never got over it? In other words, they did not yield. They allowed their creative juices to continue to flow. That is what you really want for him, right?

And a teacher who does not understand that . . . do you want that teacher to get in the way of that? [no] So, do you want to feel *good* about the teacher's misunderstanding, or do you want to feel *bad* about the teacher's misunderstanding?

Guest: I just don't want to care about what she thinks.

Abraham: Well, that is a good step. So now, you cannot change Joseph. Can you change the teacher? [no] You cannot, can you? All that effort in trying to get Joseph to be different is not going to amount to anything anyway. It is sort of all wasted effort, is it not? [yes] So why do you care? Because others make you care. The teacher calls you because the teacher wants to wield *her* power. The teacher wants to say to you, "I can't be happy when your son behaves this way, so you need to make your son behave differently." And then you want to say to the teacher, "Well, I'm sorry. I can't feel happy when you behave the way you do about the way my son behaves. So you need to change the way you're behaving about my son so that *I* can be happy."

And Joseph is the only wise one. He says, "Hey, I'm happy! You guys don't need to behave in any way to make me happy. You're out of my picture. You're a non-issue to me. I don't care what you think!" (*He* is the teacher, is he not?) So the *Emotional Journey* that you want to take is that you want to feel all right. You want to feel loving toward this teacher. You want to understand that this teacher is well-meaning. You want to say something to the teacher . . . now here, just practice this in your mind: "You know, I can't begin to tell you how nice it is to see how much you care about my little boy. It's so nice of you. So really, really, really nice of you. And I feel sorry for you because he won't listen to me either. But I've found that if I, sort of, just go with him, he's brilliant. And, as a teacher, I thought you might like to know that. And I also discovered that when I don't try to entrap him and take away his perception of freedom, he's the nicest little fellow in the world to get along with. But when I give him the impression, for even a moment, that he's not free, he fights for his life as if I'd pressed a pillow to his face. And I remember feeling that way, too. I bet you do, too.

"So I stopped putting the pillow over his face. I started flowing with the idea of his perceived freedom. And I think he's going to make us both proud if we just stay out of his way and let him be the genius that he is. And, by the way, thanks for all your trouble, and I appreciate everything you can teach him. I know he wants to learn from you. He tells me that he likes you. There are so many things you do that he enjoys. You're a good teacher. I know that you are. And I'm sorry that my little one won't conform—but I think the geniuses of the world never conformed."

And with enough conversations like that, she will stop calling you in. When she finds out that she cannot wield her power to make you make him do something that he is not going to do, she will stop calling you in, and meanwhile, Joseph will thrive, and he will win her heart, and he will show her who he is. Yes.

Guest: Thank you.

To Hopefully Move Away from Medicated Diabetes

Guest: Okay, I'm very nervous. My question is, I have diabetes. I've always believed I'd kill myself, and I feel it's a positive thing I can do, but it's like, what's preventing me from doing it?

Abraham: Well, are you just killing yourself gradually with diabetes, or are you talking about something more dramatic?

Guest: I want to just move on, just say, okay, I can do it. It is over with. But my biggest fear—

Abraham: "Move on . . . ?" Move on into a healthy physical body?

Guest: Yes. But my biggest fear is stopping medication and passing away, you know.

Abraham: Well, you are really going to hear this because the *Action Journey* says that this medication has caused you some stability. So we would encourage you to continue your *Action Journey* with no change for a while. But feel the difference between taking the medication and feeling irritation about it, and taking the medication and feeling appreciative of its temporary stabilizing faculties.

Do you understand that you are an extension of Source Energy, and that the cells of your body are summoning Life Force and they know exactly what to do? And that, as they individually and collectively communicate and *ask,* that Source Energy answers them, and that is, in fact, what happens when the doctors pronounce you alive? In other words, that is just that process.

So your cells—if you never gave any conscious attention to having diabetes or not having diabetes—the cells of your body know what to do to maintain your physical vessel to perfection. And if you are not doing something that gets in the way of that, then your body percolates along just fine. The cells talk to each other. If there is a little imbalance, they make the adjustment. Everything works perfectly.

Sometimes you are even inspired to eat different things because your cells are asking for something that that particular food would contain and, at some level of your Being, you know that your chemical factory can digest it and provide the nutrient that this particular body of cells is asking for. It is an amazing process, your physical body.

So when you are in this state where you have been diagnosed with diabetes, and you have been experiencing it long enough that it is annoying to you and cumbersome to you, you have two concurrent journeys, as everyone does at all times: You have the physical journey of dealing with your physical body, and then you have the *Emotional Journey* of how you feel about what you are dealing with.

And so, many times, it has been a longtime point of confusion, for people say, "Are you teaching non-action? Since you're teaching us that thoughts create, then where does *action* fit in with it?" And we say, action is the joyous way you live your life experience. We are not guiding you away from action.

Someone implied that there is a difference between the physical world of action, physical manifestation, and that which is Spiritual. And we want to say to you that everything that is in your environment is an extension of Source—*everything is Spiritual.*

So often, physical Beings think that we are trying to move you away from action, that it should be only thought. And then they think, *I should be able to fix my body with my thought. I should not need this medication. I'm going about it in a backwards way.* And what we want you to understand is that you are where you are, and where you are is just fine. And the *Action Journey* that you are upon, we would not upset that apple cart for anything. We would continue to take that medication. We would continue to offer that action just as you are—but we would begin to give serious attention to our *Emotional Journey.*

Just like the woman with arthritic hips, she can have arthritis in her hips and feel fearful, or she can have arthritis in her hips and feel hopeful. The difference between the fear and the hope makes the difference between whether that pain is going to leave her anytime soon, you see.

So do not worry about what you are doing with the action. You are here, you are in this body, you are taking the medication, and that is just fine. Do not condemn yourself for however you got here, or for wherever you are. We so much want you all to hear that: *Where you are is where you are—and where you are is just fine!*

Do you know anyone who has recovered?

Guest: No, I don't, but I want to be the first if there hasn't been.

Abraham: Do you know that there are people who have recovered? Do you know that there are people who have dramatically reduced their dependence on the medication? Do you know that there are people who have changed their vibration enough so that their body has once again begun producing the insulin that they want? Do you know that they are out there? So you could say, "Well, Universe, I would like you to deliver to me some documentation about that. I am looking forward to receiving some information that justifies my feeling of hopefulness." Because when most people say, "I want to be the first," the words are empty and hollow because they do not really believe that they can be the first. So did you feel relief? Did you feel some relief when we told you that there are these people?

Guest: Yes.

Abraham: And did you feel some hopefulness that you might be able to receive some information that might make you feel even more belief? [yes] And so, what just happened here is, you became hopeful about legitimately being hopeful, which is the same thing as being hopeful. You became hopeful about being hopeful, you see. Your Energy shifted.

So if someone were to walk in the door right now, meet you for the first time, and say, "Hey, how are you?" what would you say and mean?

Guest: Great! I'm doing better. I'm doing better.

Abraham: And what other words would you offer? If they said, "Well, how do you *really* feel?" what would you say?

Guest: I'm looking forward to the days that come. I'm looking—

Abraham: In other words, "I'm hopeful!"

Guest: Yes.

Abraham: "I'm hopeful." *Now, if you wanted to take it a little further, and now is as good a time as any to do that. . . .* So you are hopeful. When you say, "Looking forward to the days that follow," what do those days feel like? "Coming into alignment. My physical body's coming into alignment. I go get a test. I'm given acknowledgment that things are changing. I'm encouraged to stay on the medication, and that doesn't discourage me at all, because Abraham encouraged that, too. And I realize that I can keep that up. So I've got this blessed, wonderful insulin that's keeping me in this place of physical stability while I'm taking this *Emotional Journey*. I'm not only hopeful, I'm downright optimistic! I can see how things could change around for me. And it's pretty thrilling to think about things turning around for me, because I could be one of those medical miracles that nobody really understands—only, I understand! I took an *Emotional Journey*. I deliberately tended to the way I feel.

"I got up every morning. I meditated a little. I took a walk. I did things that made me feel good. I did things that please me. I got on rampages of appreciation. I made myself feel good on purpose because I finally understand, for the first time in my life, that the way I feel is the key to the gate between whether or not the cells of my body receive what they're asking for. And finally, I did what I said I was going to do. I got myself out of the way! I'm out of the way. I'm allowing the Well-Being to flow through me.

"And now I'm anticipating what that means: I'm going to come into physical alignment. I'm going to begin to reduce my body weight. It's going to be obvious to people who surround me. My attitude's improved already; they'll notice that right away. But they're going to begin to see some visible evidence of the improvement in my physical body. And the doctors will take tests, and big whoopee, they'll feel better, or they won't. And I'll look in the mirror and I'll feel better.

"But most of all, I'm looking forward to this life that I came forth to live. I want to live, and I want to thrive. And I can see now that I can do that. I don't have to do it all at once; I don't have to figure it out all at once. I just have to figure out, right now, how to feel a little better than I was usually feeling, right now, how to feel a little better than I was usually feeling.

"I'm going to start talking it up. I'm not going to talk it down. I'm not going to hang around with people who want to talk about what-is. I'm going to hang around with people who will get off the subject altogether, or they will talk about things that feel good to me when I talk about it. I don't need anybody's pity. I don't need anybody to help me justify where I am. I'm no longer going to use any of this stuff as an excuse for why things aren't working for me. Things are going to start working for me!"

There, you are done.

Guest: Thank you, thank you. I'm sorry it was like pulling teeth.

Abraham: You feel pretty hopeful to us. How does he seem to you? If you saw him on the street, what would you say? "Hey, you look hopeful! I can see hopefulness radiating out of you. What do you call yourself?" "Hopeful." "What did I get when I visited Abraham? I got hopeful." "When was the most significant turning point in your life?" "The day I went from fear to hope; I remember that day. I got hopeful, never to return to despair again. That was the turning point for me. That's the day I became hopeful." And that makes all the difference, yes.

Why Aren't There Abraham Teachings in Egypt?

Guest: Thank you for giving me this opportunity. I'm a little nervous, but I have a question. I'm from a different part of the world from where the Vibrational System seems to be a little low or a little bit closed. I'm from Egypt, from the Middle East, and I'm wondering why there aren't opportunities for people in the Middle East or in Egypt to have Abraham, or groups like Abraham, to provide them with opportunities of seeing other ways of living, other ways of thinking, other ways of being. Why isn't this sort of spirituality being expanded and shared with parts of the world that need healing?

Abraham: Well, the thing is, if someone, or a lot of people, or just one person in Egypt is asking, then Source Energy is answering. So the question is not, "Why is it not being offered?" The question is, *Why is it not being received?* And we want to soothe you a little bit by saying to you that, at one time, that particular region of the world was experiencing more personal enlightenment than the rest of the world all put together. In other words, Egypt is not a place that is devoid of Connection with Source Energy.

So we would not spend any more time beating the drum of "Why isn't something better?" We would begin, from your vantage point, *imagining it being better.* In other words, it only takes one here and another here and another here.

Esther was just someone who was bipping along living happily ever after who happened to be married to someone who had insatiable questions. He never stopped asking questions. He has written more questions for himself today than the rest of you put together, or nearly so. In other words, he will peruse his notes; he will contemplate them; he will listen to this again; he will talk to Esther about it. In other words, this seminar, as far as Jerry is concerned, has only just now begun. He will whittle it down; he will make an edited version; he will make a longer raw version of this seminar. . . . It will be sent to someone in Colorado who will transcribe it word for word. He will receive it back. He will read every single word of it. And still, his questions will not be satisfied, because with every answer (wonderful answers that they are) is another question that is bubbling up from within, you see.

So we want you to accept that there would be no ending to the answers that are forthcoming, and no ending to the new questions that are coming. No place on this planet is being deprived of that Connection.

So here is Esther. Now at first, when, through a process of meditation, she realized that she was receiving, and that brilliance was flowing through her . . . in the beginning, it was really startling to her because she could not believe it. Jerry recorded everything that Abraham has ever said. And Esther would hear it back, and she just could not believe that those words had flowed through her. She could not believe that that clarity had flowed through her about things that she really did not know that much about, you see.

And so she made Jerry (because it seemed very weird to her) promise that he would not ever tell anyone. She did not care how wonderful it was; she did not want anyone to know how weird she was. And we think that that is the saddest part about all of this, because what that says is, those who have somehow stumbled upon the process that allows them to open to the Energy that creates worlds, allow that God Force to flow through them, and to talk about enlightenment, are afraid because they are different from everyone else. They think that it is something that should be kept a secret. In other words, that is a big part of what keeps more people from having direct contact. You are made fun of.

So many people are afraid to be who they really are because when they are who they really are, they are so secure that the insecure ones around them try to keep them from being secure. Those who *do not* know just continue to outnumber those who *do* know, until those who know refuse to admit that they know. And in time, you have an epidemic of those who *seem* not to know, and then you say, "Why don't they know?" And we say, they knew. And they can know again. It just takes one or two here and there. And so, worry not. The word is out.

Guest: So what role could I play, as an individual who lives here, who goes back and sees that people, the majority, are holding on to a religion that is misinterpreted and that is lowering the vibration in the society?

Abraham: We say this to all teachers and uplifters, and you certainly are that: *If your vibration is here in a place of knowing and trusting and feeling good, and you have a student who is in a place of despair or fear—no matter how good your words are, they cannot hear them because the vibrational difference is too far.*

So what you do is, you acclimate to a place that is more suited to you, and you *trust*. And this is the part where the *hope* comes in. You trust that the teachers who are closer, vibrationally, to where they are can get their attention and make them hear. And then the teachers who are closer to where they *now* are can get their attention and make them hear. . . .

This is the Leading Edge of thought! In other words, this arena, while it is so satisfying *to you,* is not all that satisfying to most. There is never a crowd on the Leading Edge. But that does not mean that where everybody else is, is not just fine. Do not beat up on yourself for not being up here in joy all of the time. Make peace with where you are, and then it can get better.

And so, that is what we would say if we were talking to them. We would try to soothe them. We would try to say, you are doing all right. We would not condemn them as backwards or in the dark. We would not give them a label of *lower* vibration. We would say that it is a *different* vibration. We would say that they are still asking. We would step back and acknowledge who they really are: They are still seeking.

There is not one right lifestyle on this planet. In other words, we would not begin to profess that *our* method of teaching is more effective, more valuable, more powerful, more important, or more right than "Sai Baba's"—but it *is* different. You see?

Guest: Thank you very much. I appreciate this, thank you.

Abraham: Yes, indeed.

Wants a Million Dollars Without Working for It

Guest: Hello, Abraham. I've heard you say, on several tapes, that we don't live in an assertive world. We can bring everything to us by our thoughts. So . . .

Abraham: There is no assertion.

Guest: How can I balance wanting to draw everything into my life without having to go into the doing or the being of whatever it is I do? I want to create a million dollars, but I don't want to go to work for it.

Abraham: Well, your statement is really telling and really important, because what you are saying is, "I want a million dollars, and I believe that there are ways to get a million dollars that I don't want to do." So what you are doing is saying, "I want this, but I don't want *this.*" And that is not a very powerful state of being, because you are setting up a contradiction right away.

So you soften that by saying, "I want a million dollars, and I want to find a way that is compatible with me to receive it." There is less resistance in that. You say, "I want a million dollars, and I know that there are a lot of people who have a million dollars, who got it in a way that would *not* be uncomfortable to me." But when you say, "I want a million dollars, but there's no one I'm going to inherit it from," or "I want a million dollars, but nobody that I know is going to die and leave it to me. . . ." In other words, you need to stop the contradiction.

When you talk about *what* you want and *why* you want it, there is usually less resistance within you than when you talk about what you want and *how* you are going to get it. Because when you pose questions that you do not have answers for, like *how, where, when,* and *who,* it sets up a contradictory vibration within you that slows everything down.

Feel how resistance free this statement is: "There must surely be many people on this planet today who have a million dollars, and in excess of it, who at one time were standing right where I am. They just wanted it, but had no idea how it was going to come."

Words like *faith* and *trust* are so annoying on some levels, but we want to explain their value, because even though you do not know *how* or *where* or *when* or *who,* if you know <u>what,</u> and you have talked about <u>why</u> you want it and you have practiced the thought of it until it is starting to feel very familiar to you, what begins to happen is that things that before now could not happen to you . . . begin happening. Ideas that would not even occur to you, before, now begin to occur to you, and interactions with people that you do not have access to now . . . begin to happen. And when your million and many more come to you, you will wonder where it always was.

Guest: I was wondering if I was trying to create something that was too big, and the gap between what I wanted and where I am was too big, and that was causing some of the grief?

Abraham: Well, surely a million dollars is not too big from where you stand. That is just not too big. Esther was listening to the words that a billionaire entrepreneur chose, words like, "Oh, it's a juggernaut. Oh, it's a sure success. Oh, it's the most sensational building that's ever been built. We're building the most beautiful building in Chicago that has ever been built. Oh, this is magnificent. Oh yes, *that* person's a friend of mine." And as she listened, she began to realize that he had figured it out. Now, he annoys most of the world, but you know what? He does not care! He has developed a relationship between what he wants and where he is.

Even when what he wanted and where he was were not in the same place, you would not know it to hear him tell it. In other words, he continues to tell the story the way he <u>wants</u> it to be—so the Universe continues to yield to him. Now there are all kinds of people who say, "Oh, he's a braggart. Oh, of course *he* can talk like that; he's a billionaire." And we say, he was not always. He talked like that—and *then* he became that.

So you do not have to follow his lifestyle or his personality. But you *do* have to follow the success principles that he has found: *You have to talk about what you <u>want.</u> You have to tell it like you <u>want</u> it to be. You cannot face reality as it is and have reality change in any way. You have to face the parts of reality that you love and fill in the gaps with things that you get from your imagination, or from your expectation.*

So here you are, and you have a lot of good things in your life, which you accentuate, talk about, appreciate, and make lists of. You make lists of *Positive Aspects,* and you get on *Rampages of Appreciation.* You look for good wherever you see it, and you feel good as much as you can.

Then you have goals and you do not know how you are going to achieve them. So then you fill those in with imagination, visualization, and pretending, and then as you start doing that, you will have a dream about it that makes it feel more real. Or you will meet somebody who is really living that way. Or you will turn on the television and somebody will be talking just like you have been imagining. Or you will pick up a book, or you will hear another interview. . . . In other words, *the Universe will help you rendezvous with whatever the vibration is that you have finally achieved.*

The Universe does not know the difference between someone who has a million dollars and someone who just feels like they have a million dollars. And when you feel like you have it, your vibration is such that the Law of Attraction must line you up with things like that. And that is true whether you are talking about relationships, the building of empires, attracting people to help you in your business. . . . It does not matter what it is—you have to find the vibration of it, and you have to practice the vibration of it until the vibration of your desire supersedes the vibration of doubt. When the vibration of your desire supersedes your vibration of doubt, bam! It happens. And then you say, "Where have you been?"

You say, "I knew you were coming. I could *feel* you. At first, I just felt *hopeful* that you'd be there. But eventually, I started really *trusting* that you'd be there. And then, not very long ago, I *knew* you'd be there, and [plunk], there you are." But the things you want cannot come until you achieve that knowing, and that knowing does not come easily because you have been practicing *not* knowing.

You are often not willing to admit how you feel because you are worried about what somebody else might say about how you feel. So you really have to get to the place where you do not talk so much to people who do not understand. You talk to those who *do* understand—or you just keep your own counsel.

Jerry wrote a paper years ago that said: *Keep your ideas to yourself until they are fully developed,* because he saw so many people whom he was counseling in business, whom he would see get fired up over an idea, but it was a new idea to them, and they had not practiced it long enough that it was dominant within them. It was tentative within them (and he knew that it could go either way), and then they would go home and talk to somebody about their new idea before it was really shored up within them. And that person and their doubt and their negative commentary would activate that old vibration within this person, and then it was all over, because the seed of their financial abundance had not been allowed to germinate and get enough of a foothold that it was strong on its own.

There is no reason for you to experience anything less than what you want. If you have the ability to imagine it, this Universe has the ability to give it to you. Knowing it, knowing that you want it, *asking for it,* is *Step One* and *Step Two,* because you have asked, and the Universe has given—now, you just have to get out of the way and let it in.

One more thing we want to say to you: When you say you want it but you do not want to work for it, we think that is where your cross-purpose is: You do not like doing the things that you think you are going to have to do in order to get it, but you do not believe you can get it otherwise. That is where the contradiction is.

What you are saying to the Universe is: "Do this *impossible* thing." So what you have to do is find some way of not making it feel impossible. Do a little research. Notice how many different ways there are for money to come in. In other words, give yourself some reason to believe that it is possible for you to receive.

Guest: Okay. Thank you very much.

Abraham: Yes, indeed.

Have We Any Responsibility to Save Others?

Guest: My question is about *responsibility.* I've heard you indicate that it's about taking care of ourselves; however, do we not have a responsibility to help people whom we're able to help?

Abraham: We love the brilliant choice of words that you offered. "Do we not have a responsibility to help people whom we are able to help?" If you are vibrating here, and they are vibrating *here,* you do not have much to offer them. In other words, if they are not somewhere within your vibrational vicinity, they cannot hear you.

And so, a teacher, an uplifter, a healer, a helper, is only as effective as his ability to understand where the person he is wanting to help is vibrating. So you want to adjust your vibration, as close as you can, without losing your balance. In other words, it is a matter of staying in vibrational alignment with the Energy that you will use to help them, without dipping out of it.

So the "responsibility" of all of this (you might not like this in light of your question, but we do) really lies with the *Law of*

Attraction. Sometimes people talk about justice or injustice. And we say that *there is never injustice, because nothing can ever happen to anyone that is different from the vibration that they are offering.* The greatest value that you could offer to others (and you can call it a responsibility if you like) is to help them understand that they are the creator of their own experience, and that they are offering a vibration, and that the vibration that they offer is what is netting the results they are getting. Then teach through the clarity of your example.

Guest: What would you call that? If I didn't call that *responsibility,* what would you call that?

Abraham: *Teaching through the clarity of my example.* We would call it *compassionate acknowledgment of the power of everyone.* We would call it *alignment with who I am so that I see the beauty and the power in everyone I focus upon.* We would call it *alignment with Source and understanding of individual power.* We would call it *belief in your ability to achieve anything you want to achieve.* We would call it *the power to see your value, even when you do not.* We would call it *the power to know your wellness, even if you are sick.* We would call it *the power to know your prosperity, even when you cannot pay your bills.* We would call it *the power to think about you in the way that feels best to me so that I can connect with Source and flood who you are through my vantage point.* We would call it *the most responsible, compassionate utilization of Source Energy that exists anywhere in the Universe.*

Guest: Thank you.

Must Children Be Influenced to Feel Inappropriate?

Guest: Good morning, and thank you so very much, Esther and Jerry and Abraham. It's been about ten months since I was exposed to the first recording, and my life has changed. And my question is, where have you been all my life?

Abraham: In vibrational escrow (fun!) just on the other side of the curtain, waiting for it to open.

Guest: Of course I knew that answer because I listen to your tapes nonstop, so to speak. But here it is: The last conversation we had, two weeks ago, I said I didn't want to come back here. And you said, huh, tough luck. You have no choice.

Abraham: Where is the scribe (fun!)? You are paraphrasing, of course.

Guest: Yes.

Abraham: Well, that is really what we *meant*. You were right.

Guest: Yes, yes. So, before we came here, I said, "I want to come to this life, to this world, and line up this vibration and create this fabulous life." And then I come here, like you said, and then we end up in this (many times, not always) incredible negative environment that makes us (or however this works) forget all these wonderful things we knew before we came. So, I'm . . .

Abraham: We understand. We have this conversation from time to time with people, and we always appreciate it when there is someone very intense in this thought that gives us an opportunity to maybe say it in new ways.

Before you came forth into this physical body, you were not so much saying, "I'm going to jump into this time-space reality, and I'm going to be able to find my way within a harsh environment." You felt utterly eager to jump in. You felt utterly confident.

It is the difference between that feeling of sure-footedness—that feeling of confidence and eagerness—and that feeling of fear. So it is hard for you to remember confidence from a place of fear, or to remember exhilaration and passion from a place of anger. They are different vibrations.

We could talk a long time, and we could not really make any headway, because when you are in the place of seeing the world as a hard place or a negative place or an evil place or as an uncomfortable place or an unkind place . . . when that has been what you have been focused upon (and with good reason; we are certainly not suggesting that you made it up just to be hard on yourself), you cannot hear these words about the other.

Yet we keep wanting to tell you to at least accept at face value that you really were in this vibration of eagerness when you made the decision to come forth into physical. So you say, "Okay, I get that. I was eager *then*. I wanted to come forth. Why did it change?" And we want to say to you that it changed because you were surrounded by others who had already forgotten that the way *they* feel matters—who had already begun to use *outside* circumstances and *outside* guidance to help them make the decisions about how they would gravitate with their thoughts.

Esther turned on the television, checking out the new satellite dishes in the new monster bus, a day or two ago, and saw a television psychologist counseling a young man. It was so brutal that Esther had to turn off the TV. This counselor was badgering this young man (who, as a young boy, had sexual intimacy with another child). Then, years later, he had lied about it on a lie detector. And now he was being badgered. Why would he not admit his evil and his wrongdoing, because admitting must surely be the first stage in all of that.

Esther just walked away from it and turned it off. She thought, *There are so many rules and so many mind-sets of the way you should behave, so many people ready to stand and judge you as inappropriate if you do not jump through their hoops in the way they think that they need you to so that they can feel better. . . . So many people have gotten so separated from their own sense of Well-Being.*

Esther wished that she could jump inside the television and just put her arms around this young boy and say, "Don't listen to them; you're not bad!" She wanted so much to tell him that *they* don't know who you are. Don't listen to them.

So our answer to you is that so many of you have begun to listen to those in authority around you, rather than listening to the Guidance that you were born with. Now, the next logical question would be: "Well, shouldn't it be set up differently? Shouldn't our Guidance come through clearer?" And we say that your Guidance is very clear: *You know what feels good. You know what feels bad.* You can reach back to some of your earliest memories and remember that first gut-wrenching feeling that you got when somebody was pointing to you and calling you inappropriate.

We would imagine that many of you could sit down and make a list of those kinds of experiences, where, little by little, someone tried to convince you that you were not good. And, in every case, it was someone who had already convinced themselves that *they* were not good, you see.

So what we want to say is that you were born with Guidance. And now what we are hearing from so many of you is, "But why didn't I use the Guidance I was born with?" But rather than saying, "Why didn't I use the Guidance I was born with?" we would so much rather hear from you, "I'm going to begin to use the Guidance that I was born with." And then what happens is that you then stand in this powerful place where you have extracted all of this contrasting experience that has launched incredible rockets of desire into your future. And now, as you come into alignment, most of you, in nearly every case, say, *Every bit of that stuff that yesterday I said was horrible, I now feel appreciation for—because it gave me the clarity to desire. Now I am the receiver of that which I have desired, and my life is more because of it than it would have been otherwise.*

So the conversation that we want to have with you is not whether the system is right or not (it is). The conversation we want to have with you is, "How can I, in my *now,* close the gap between my asking and receiving? How can I become so entrusting of the Laws of the Universe, and so aware of my own vibrational countenance, that I can get into this place where I just *expect* Well-Being to flow to me?"

When you get to that place, that eagerness returns. That is exactly how the little ones feel. Watch them. Jerry and Esther were in a Subway sandwich shop a day or two ago in Oregon. Esther was in line waiting her turn. Jerry had taken a seat in one of the booths and was enjoying his moment while watching Esther in line, and also watching a family waiting in line ahead of her. There was a father and a mother (the mother holding a small one), and a little girl who looked to be about four years old.

So the little girl feels Jerry's appreciation of her and turns and looks at him and smiles. He smiles back. Then she sneaks behind the counter and peeks around at him. And then he hides behind his hat. And then she sneaks around again, and he hides behind the table. And then she meows like a cat, and he barks like a dog. Her parents now have their sandwiches and they are taking them to-go, and while her parents are looking the other way, the little girl rushes up to Jerry, but he does not stand up. She hugs his shoulder, lays her head right on him, gives him just a squeeze, and then off she goes.

And Esther said, "She's still in that place of knowing Well-Being. She's in vibrational alignment with who she is, and she recognized a vibrational equivalent." She is tuned in, tapped in, turned on, and apparently lives in an environment where she had not been taught to "stay away from strangers; strangers are bad." She apparently lives in an unguarded environment where she is still able to follow her heart.

So we do not care if you are three or four, still following your heart, and then you forget how to do that for a while, and then you rediscover, because the feeling of coming back into alignment with who you are is an undeniable experience. And once you *consciously* make it, you never have to leave it again, you see.

So the question that we are really hearing is, "Why does it happen?" We say, stuff happens. You say, "But shouldn't it be different?" And we say, no, it's perfect. And you say, "But shouldn't my *Guidance System* have been stronger?" And we say, it is as strong as it ever needs to be. It is not a controller; it is *Guidance.* You say, "But shouldn't I have been born into a better environment?" We say, you would not be who you are if you had been. You say, "But shouldn't it have been easier along the way?" We say yes, but that was up to you. You say, "But shouldn't it be easier now?" And we say yes, but that is up to you.

In other words, we can sit here today and continue the struggle the rest of your physical life, or we can say, *Let's make peace with it.*

Guest: Well, I'm out of the struggle. My next question is, most of us have been struggling for so long, and it seems like it's a secret, this *Law of Allowing,* this Vibrational Match. Why is it such a secret?

Abraham: Well, the secret is out (fun!). But it has never been a secret. It has been a willingness to trust somebody else over the way you feel. It is a by-product of being born as a little person into a family of big people who think that they have the answers, or who want to protect you. But it is also a function of, from your Broader Non-Physical Perspective, wanting the contrasting experience in order to help you formulate your desires.

You see, you have to grasp this: This is an evolving, expanding Universe. This is not a Universe where somebody has it all figured out, where here is a group of angels in heaven who have figured out the perfect life, and then they say, "Go forth little ones and just live as *we've* been living." It is not that way. *There must be expansion in order for there to continue to be existence.*

And so, with expansion comes contrast, and with contrast comes discernment; with contrast comes the ability to speculate, to mold, to anticipate. Look at it this way: If you were a chef in a well-stocked kitchen, you would be so much happier than if you were a chef in a kitchen that only had three ingredients. In other words, a well-stocked kitchen does not mean that you have to put it *all* in your pie, but it sure does give you a lot of other options, you see.

So that is really why. Make peace with it. Say, "This contrasting world is what the expansion is all about. The variety, the contrast, is what puts the Eternalness in Eternity. And we were always born with Guidance." And lament only for a little bit that you lost sense of your Guidance. We do not think that any of you have lost sense of it as much as you think. We think you know when your feelings are hurt. We think you know when you are angry. We think you know when you feel disempowered. We think you know it.

And we think that it is time for you to take it back. But we think that it is also time for you to reach the place where you really take it back. As long as you are blaming anyone or anything for anything, you are disempowered. And we are not just talking to you; we are talking to anyone—*as long as you are blaming anyone or anything for anything, you are disempowered. Because that says that they have power over me. And no one does, because no one can vibrate for you.*

The *Law of Attraction* is lovingly delivering to everyone who asks, the precise answer that they are able to hear. So, never suffer over those who are not getting your answers, because you cannot even force-feed them. We gave that up a long time ago. *As teachers, we have come to understand that we are only as effective as our understanding of where our student is.*

So, we let the *Law of Attraction* bring those who are ready for *this,* and we trust that the *Law of Attraction* is bringing all others to what *they* are ready for. And they are not suffering in the way you think they are suffering. They are not you.

He Is Most Appreciative of His Success

Guest: Hello. Thank you so much for calling on me. We got to bed early and I realized, as I went to sleep, that I could see you calling on me. I felt that *feeling,* and I just appreciate it so much; you've helped us so much in our lives that everything that has happened since we have met you has been 180 degrees different than it was before.

Abraham: Good things have been on their way to you for a long time, because you want them and you have been deserving of them. All that we did was speed up the *allowing* process a little bit.

Guest: Thank you for that. I wanted to do a little bit of a *Rampage of Appreciation* now, because what I appreciate when I listen to the tapes is when people say what they have learned and gained from this. And I want to appreciate, of course, Jerry and Esther and Abraham, the trinity (fun!), and I want to appreciate my wife, who practices what you preach, and is such a shining light of this practice. It's really what allows me to focus and create and do everything that we've been able to do—and besides that, the love of my life.

I wanted to, sort of, give some background about what happened: Before I met her (and thus, you), we went from basically being in debt to being able to buy a house with cash. My company was failing; in fact, it had fallen apart the day before I met her. And now she was able to resurrect it. In the past (it was a five-year-old company), everything I was doing, I was doing wrong. When I met her and we started putting your principles to work, the principles of *allowing* and doing the *non-action journey,* all the decisions that we made were the correct ones, and everything went right. Also, we've been able to get into alignment. I've been able to get into alignment and dispel so many of the addictions that I had that were holding me back. So I just want to appreciate all of those things.

The way that we did it, was, we listened and practiced and appreciated your teachings. We went on the cruise, which was our honeymoon, and it was right after that that we got a check for $144,000, that was just amazing. And then, we also created an environment of Well-Being, an oasis of joy. . . .

You know, I've separated from my mother's (probably good) intentions, but they've affected me in a negative way. My father's negative approach to money kept me down. Getting rid of all those things and allowing the Universe to take over and connecting to that has really been what's allowed all this to happen.

Now we just travel, and we've had a lot of beautiful experiences. All the wealth comes from that. . . . So, that's *my Rampage of Appreciation.* And the first question . . . I'm speaking to Abraham. Abraham, what is the difference between you and me?

Abraham: Nothing worth mentioning (fun!). *In your Rampage of Appreciation, you are a Vibrational Match to that which we are. And there are no differences.*

Guest: That brings tears to my eyes. It's just wonderful, that Connection. How can I strengthen my awareness of it?

Abraham: By looking for it, and not being upset if you notice that it is not there as strongly in one moment, but appreciating it when it is there in another. Until, eventually, the drum that you will be beating is that of the Connection. And then, it will be odd, really odd, when it is *not* there.

Guest: That resistance, when it is not there, is that somehow related to time? Is time equal to resistance?

Abraham: Not really. *Time* is another subject. It is not necessary to have resistance just because you have come forth into a time-space reality. But it is natural that out on the Leading Edge of anything, that there would be more resistance than not out on the Leading Edge. In other words, there is a comfort zone that is back from the Leading Edge that is not present on the Leading Edge.

It ties in with something that you said earlier, that we want to talk about, when you were talking about how everything is going so well, and how all of the answers to the questions are coming, and everything is unfolding so perfectly. And we love hearing that from you. But we want to remind you that you cannot get it wrong, and you never get it done. So relax and allow yourself some leeway in all of this.

In other words, sometimes (and we can feel it with you), it's a common thing when you go from *not allowing* as intensely as you now are, to suddenly putting a few pieces into place and *allowing* (as happened when the two of you came together) what happens: Sometimes you then try to hold yourself to some strict, and maybe even unnatural, standard of wanting to maintain the momentum, or wanting to keep the perfection. And then you freak out a little bit if you are not able to do that, as if you might somehow turn back to what was before.

We want you to relax and know that you cannot turn back. You have come too far. But you might lapse into a little less *allowing* from time to time, and that is just fine. In other words, what this creative endeavor is about, that you are so firmly upon, is new contrast, which produces new desire, which is strange at first, but then you align to it. And then, in the alignment, more movement happens, and then a new platform produces new opportunity for new questions and new desires, which feel strange at first, but then you align to it. . . .

In other words, you will never *not* understand how it works. But you will not necessarily always be in the perfect place at the perfect time—but that is part of the fun; that is part of the adventure. It will always become what you want it to be—and quickly. And, more assuredly, it will be quick if you can relax in whatever comes.

We have been enjoying watching Jerry and Esther, in that vein, in that they no longer feel responsible for living the perfect life. And we have helped them by spewing, workshop after workshop, every time they screw up (fun!). We do not hold them up as perfect role models; we hold them up as people in love with each other and with life, who are out there having new experiences that they are constantly adjusting to, who feel really good, mostly, and not so good, rarely, who know what to do when they feel not so good. So that takes the pressure off. They are always finding their balance, as any talented artist does. *You are always reaching for balance. Just know that you will always find it, so you do not freak out when you are out of balance.*

Guest: That's great. Thank you.

Wants to Love Her Fun-Self More

Guest: I am so excited. . . . My question, my desire, even from this *now* place—how do I love myself more? How do I bring myself to feel more worthy and deserving and have more fun? And already I feel much closer to that.

Abraham: Well, a big piece of it has already fallen into place because everyone naturally loves themselves. There is nothing more natural than for you to feel the way you feel. And the *you* we are talking about is that *Source-Energy You* that came forth lovingly into this experience, who loves what it sees. In other words, the essence of you, the Energy of you, the soul or Source of you, is love. And you train that out of yourself (primarily in the way that your question amplifies) in that you worry about what this one and that one and this one and that one think of you.

How do I love myself? The answer to that is . . . just stop *not* liking yourself. In other words, *love is the natural state of being if you are not pushing against something unwanted.*

Comparison is an interesting thing, because it is necessary in order to define preference. But can you feel the difference between looking at all of these things and saying *yes* to this, and looking at all of these things and saying, *no, no, no, no, no?*

We have been talking about Energy Balancing, and we want you to realize that whatever you give your attention to activates a vibration, so when you look at a buffet of things and you say *yes,* it activates it. *Yes,* it activates it. *Yes,* it activates it. If you are saying *yes* to the things that you want, then you have activated things that you want, and you are offering a vibration only about what you want, and Source Energy is answering that. Now, everything is flowing comfortably.

But in this Universe where it is all about attraction, there is no assertion, there is no exclusion. You cannot say *no* to something and make it go away When you say *no* to it, it comes, *because attention to it <u>asks</u> for it,* or activates the equivalent within you, which is the same thing as asking for it. So when you look at a buffet of things wanted and unwanted and you say, "Well, I want that, but I don't want *that,*" you include them both. "Well, I want that, but I don't want *that.* I like this about myself, but I don't like *that* about myself." Now you have activated *all* of that. So now, instead of a clear, pure, balanced Energy (balanced meaning in alignment with Source), you are out of balance because you are introducing all this foreign stuff. And the feeling of not liking yourself is introducing a whole bunch of vibrations that do not mesh with who-you-really-are. So the feeling of not liking yourself or someone else, the feeling of anti-love, is the feeling of introducing vibrations that do not allow a pure Connection with the Energy that *is* love. Makes sense?

Guest: I'd like to receive for everyone, a *Rampage of Appreciation* so I can hear it in this new place of self, from the viewpoint of the Non-Physical.

Abraham: ". . . Here I am in my physical body, and I'm now consciously recognizing that I'm an extension of Source Energy. And, understanding what I'm now coming to know about Source Energy, that means that I am Pure Positive Energy and that the essence of me is all wonderful things, and that anytime I feel less than enthusiastic, eager, appreciative, or in love of self, it's because I've introduced something else unnatural to the equation.

"I'm so happy that I have a *Guidance System* within me that will point out to me, moment by moment, incrementally, anytime I may be introducing an Energy relative to myself or relative to anything that would keep me from being in balanced vibrational alignment with who-I-really-am.

"So I'm loving my *Guidance System*. I'm loving my emotions, all of them. I'm loving the ones that feel wonderful, and I'm loving the ones that don't feel so wonderful, because all of them are there to assist me in tweaking myself—moment by moment, gently, more and more, subject by subject—into vibrational alignment.

"I love that there's no race to run about this. I love that I'm an Eternal Being and that I can take my time in it. And I love that the rewards are instantaneous . . . that as I reach for something and feel good, I'm right there. And as I reach for something and don't feel so good, I can still reach for the best-feeling thought that I have access to, and that's good enough for right now. In fact, that's all I do have access to right now.

"I'm no longer going to ask myself to feel good when I feel bad. Instead, I'm just going to ask myself to feel a little better than

I'm feeling, understanding that if I feel really bad and I try to feel a *little* better, and I do, and then I still don't feel very good but I try to feel a *little* better, and do, and I still don't feel all that good, but I try to feel a *little* better, and do, and I still don't feel all that good, but I try to feel a *little* better, and I do. . . . And now, I'm feeling pretty good, but I'd like to feel better, and I do. And now, I'm feeling pretty darn good, but I'd like to feel better—and I do. And now, I'm feeling *really* good. *I am loving feeling really good, and I can hardly remember not feeling good. But I'm not worried about not feeling good because I know that if I ever do not feel good, I can just try to feel a little better—and I will.*

"And now, I'm feeling really, really good, and I'm loving it . . . I notice that that person over there is noticing that I'm feeling pretty good, and that person isn't very happy about my feeling pretty good. And so now, I don't feel as good as I felt before. But it's all right that I don't feel as good as I felt before, because I know that I can feel as good as I want to feel, and where I am is okay. And I'm not mad at that person or at me because I don't feel so good, because I know that all I have to do is try to feel a little better, and I *can* feel a little better—and I *do*.

"And now, I feel utterly free. I'm no longer afraid of not feeling good because I know how easy it is to move from not feeling very good to feeling a little better. But I'm no longer going to ask the impossible of going from not feeling good to then feeling *really* good. *I'm just going to feel a little better and a little better and a little better and a little better. And I know that there's no place that I cannot get to from there. Yes!*"

Does Our Consciousness Require Our Physical Form?

Guest: Good afternoon, Abraham. I actually have 100 questions, but I'm only going to ask 2. It's like having the genie bottle and having to think about only three wishes.

When we do emerge into Non-Physical Beings, how long do we stay there? Do some of us decide not to come back to this physical time-space?

Abraham: No, because being here is the creative excellence that you are reaching for. Your question has a little bit of a flaw at its basis because it almost assumes that you are dead *or* alive; you are physical *or* you are Non-Physical. When, in reality, you are Eternally this Non-Physical Energy that sometimes focuses some of that Energy into a physical body.

You see, someone like Abraham (we are Collective Consciousness that can flow into many of you simultaneously) does not need to be born into a body. It is sort of like saying that the electricity that flows through my house powers the toaster. And when will *all* of the electricity jump into the toaster? And we say never. That is not the way it works. In other words, the current flows to the toaster, and the toaster is the Leading-Edge experience (in our example).

So, the Non-Physical Energy that is *you* will always be that Non-Physical Energy. Some of it is focused within you in this physical body or in others, or tapping in like Abraham through an opportunity like this where many of us are participating.

Consciousness does not need physical form—but physical form needs Consciousness. And Consciousness enjoys physical form because physical form is the Leading Edge of thought. So, Consciousness expands through the physical form. It is not one or the other.

So, at the same time that your Inner Being can be flowing through you in this body and in this personality, your same Non-Physical Energy could be flowing through another. You call that "soul mates." You call that "twin flames." But you usually use it romantically, and you usually use it sparingly. *You usually assume that there are only one or two of them, but you come forth in clusters— you are Streams of Consciousness having these experiences together.*

It would be accurate to say that you are actually *soul mates* with every other physical human who is presently focused upon your planet because we *all* come forth from the same Non-Physical Energy Stream, and you *all* want experiences and exposure to one another—which stimulates the individual preference within each for the benefit of the whole, you see. Yes?

Guest: Yes, thank you.

Abraham: *It really is time for you all to get over this __death__ thing. It really is time for you to stop worrying about it, because it is inevitable—*

and it is delicious. The only thing that you really have reason to worry about is not allowing the Energy that is you to flow. In other words, feeling bad is the only thing that you ever need to worry about. And you do not need to worry about that, because you have control over feeling bad.

Esther was typing the descriptions of a recent seminar, and there was one description of a mother who was suffering over the death of her son and blaming herself for not having been a better mother. As Esther typed those words, she got just a wafting in her stomach of how that must feel, and how awful that pressure must be, and how awful it is to feel terrible about something and believe that you cannot do anything about it. In other words, this woman's son was dead; she couldn't bring him back. She believed that she would never be happy again because he was dead. In other words, that is the ultimate fear of death, is it not . . . the feeling that something bad will happen to someone I love, and I will never be able to get my happy self back to where I want to be.

Then Esther remembered having had an experience herself that felt so awful. She also remembered having other experiences, later, where she worried that something might happen that would make her feel that bad again. And then she remembered being surprised and amazed and delighted that she never, ever felt that bad again. She remembered attracting the knowledge that there is no reason to ever feel bad again. So she said to Jerry (he did not know what she was talking about, but she just sort of called out from the other end of the coach), "I love knowing that I never have to feel bad again!"

In other words, so many people are waiting for the other shoe to drop. Their lives feel good to them, but they are worried that something will happen that will take that good feeling away. And we want to say to all of you, nothing like that can ever happen to you once you understand, and once you remember, *you get to choose how you focus; therefore, you get to choose how you feel.*

No one will ever lose their fear of death until they discover their power to live. . . . And no one will really discover their power to live (and by that we mean live in joy) until they have control of their vibration. . . . And no one really ever has control of their vibration until they make the association between how they feel and what their vibration is. . . . And no one will ever be able to control the way they feel until they show themselves that anger feels better than fear, and that frustration feels better than anger—and that they *do* have the power to direct a thought to feel a little better.

When you show yourself that you can feel a little better—you cannot jump from here to *here*, you cannot jump from fear all the way to joy, but you can jump incrementally—you regain your power. And when you regain that knowledge, your fear of all things, including death, will dissipate.

Guest: Thank you, Abraham.

Heiress's Son Isn't Speaking to His Mother

Guest: Okay. I'm in a really exciting place in my life right now. My parents have died, and I'm not communicating with the rest of my family. So, there's nobody left to push my buttons. I've been doing the *Emotional Journey,* like, two hours a day. Not because I have to, but because I love it. I'm so excited to get up and start it, you know? And it changed so many things in my life. I feel like I'm starting my life all over again. . . .

My son isn't speaking to me because he believes I'm blowing all my money (I don't have medical insurance) so there'll be nothing for him after I go, and that I'm going to get sick, and I'm going to go into the hospital, and I'm going to blow all the money. So he's not speaking to me. I love my son, and I've done the *Emotional Journey* on that, and I feel pretty good about that. Except I just wondered if there's any advice for me, because I would really love to have a relationship with him.

Abraham: Well, we would say to our children if we were standing in your physical shoes, "There is a vortex that will allow all that you want to flow. And you do not need anything that has flowed through *my* vortex to be the stuff of *yours.*" And then we would say, "If you're not speaking to me because you're worried that there will be no inheritance, then your thoughts are valid. (Fun!) Because I don't believe that an inheritance is good for you. I think finding your own way is good for you." And then he would say, "But *you* have an inheritance. Why shouldn't your inheritance pass on to me?" And then we would say to him, "Because you have access to the Stream of Well-being, and I want so much for you to experience the thrill of deciding you want something, opening your vortex, and letting it flow in. I don't want your happiness to be dependent upon me. I don't want your happiness to be dependent upon anyone. And so, you're right, son. I'm doing my level best to make sure that my money and me all come to an end on the same day."

Then when he realizes that you are serious, he can make his own decisions about how much he wants to talk with you—or not. But do you really want a relationship that is based on how much he is going to get from you after you die?

Guest: No, no.

Abraham: Do you really want a relationship that is based on how much stuff is going to come to you? In other words, the relationship that you want to have with anyone is based upon *your* alignment with Source and *their* alignment with Source.

Guest: See, that's all he knows. Money has always come to him.

Abraham: Well then, it always will.

Guest: Through my family, and then through me . . . so, that's all he sees. But I'll try talking to him.

Abraham: Well, you see what is happening? And this is a really good thing to discuss, because, what he is living is a very exaggerated example of what a lot of people feel. It is a very strong distortion, but a lot of people believe that there is a finite amount of wealth. In other words, "There's so much in this trust fund that all of us are sharing, and if mother goes crazy and spends more of it, then there will be too little left for me." People feel that way about resources in general: "If someone is rich, then they must be depriving someone who is poor from having more." But it just is not that way.

Your son's expectation for Well-Being, if it is in place, will always be there. But his anger at you, as he feels that you are squandering it, is holding him in a place where Well-Being cannot flow to him. So, if this has been the primary means, or the only means, through which his Well-Being is flowing, it is drying up—not because of your behavior, but because of his response to your behavior. And whether he will learn that through something that you will say or not is questionable. Usually, words do not teach.

Guest: Okay, thank you very much.

Satisfied with _What-Is_, or Jealous of Others?

Guest: Hi. How are you today? It's a beautiful day, huh?

Abraham: Yes. We are extremely well. Words cannot describe it.

Guest: Wow. First, I'd like to express some appreciation for you and your message. I find it really uplifting and reassuring, and the daily quotes on your Website are great, because you made my day many times. You know, I need it in the morning. And also, I don't know Jerry and Esther, really, but they seem like really, really great people, and humble in every sense of the word. Because, you know, you could, theoretically, just cater "to the stars," you know what I mean, instead of us normal people?

Abraham: Their desire is an expansion of the message, so their intent is to stand in an environment where as many people like you as possible can come forth with your unique perspective and reach into Infinite Intelligence in a way that has not been reached before. That is what rings their bells—and ours. Yes.

Guest: Great. I was wondering about the perfect stance that you're talking about, in _being happy with where I am and eager for more._ The problem that I have sometimes (Not all the time. Maybe it's all the time, but who knows?) is that when I see someone who is further along than me, I can get jealous and envious. Then I'm not so happy with what _I_ have because then I, kind of, want what _they_ have. And I don't want to begrudge other people their fortune.

Even, for instance, famous people, when they end up in divorce, I kind of relish that a little bit, that *their* lives aren't perfect.

I'd like to be happy about other people's happiness, rather than relishing their unhappiness. Also, I hear a lot of people's stories, and when they have something negative to say, or something bad is happening to them, I kind of listen a little bit more than I do when they talk about something great happening to them, even though I've had both. But I don't want to begrudge other people their happiness and fortune, because if I can be happy about *their* fortune, that would bring me *my* fortune.

Abraham: Well, earlier you said, "Happy where I am and eager for more." So you cannot be happy where you are and *jealous* of what somebody else is doing at the same time. Those are very different frequencies. It is really to your advantage to get happy whether you do it for them or whether you do it for yourself. Very often we say to people, *Do not feel better about what somebody else is doing, to do <u>them</u> a favor; do it to do <u>yourself</u> a favor because it is an adjusting of your own vibration.*

There are a number of things that we want to tell you about this because you have stirred a lot up, and this is very important. A lot of people can relate to what you are talking about. So, let us talk about this feeling of *jealousy.*

When you are moving through your life, there are many things that life experience has helped you to realize that you want. So, when you look out into the world and you see someone else living something that you want, often what it does is point out to you the distance between where you are and where you want to be— that is what that feeling of *jealousy* is. . . . *Jealousy is an activated awareness of the difference between my own desire and my own current vibrational offering.*

So, moving up the *Emotional Guidance Scale* is necessary for you to be in a place where the discomfort of jealousy goes away. And when the discomfort of jealousy goes away, you also have achieved that Energy Balance, or that vibrational alignment, that is necessary before you can let in what you are asking for.

So, the first thing that we would say—if we found ourselves feeling the discomfort of jealousy or negative emotion—is, "Well, this is a good sign because it means that I want something. But it also means that I'm not, right now, in vibrational alignment with whatever it is that I want. And I've got to become in vibrational alignment before I can let in what I want."

We want you to care about your own balancing of Energy, so much so, that we want you to leave everybody else out of the equation. *If you are trying to achieve as much as someone out there is achieving; if you are comparing what you have accomplished with what anybody else has accomplished, it is going to drive you crazy because there is always going to be somebody else who is focused in a more succinct way on something who has managed to attract something or create something beyond what you have.*

In other words, you are never going to be in the place where you have achieved the most on all subjects that *everybody* on the planet has ever achieved. It is just not going to happen. And that is one of the reasons—not the biggest reason—but it is one of the reasons that we think it is really a good idea if you get your nose out of all of their businesses, and you put your nose in your own business. As far as we can see, your only business is your alignment of Energy. Your only business is managing the way you feel.

We know that you are not feeling negative emotion because you are jealous that somebody else has something. The negative emotion that you are feeling is because you want something that *you* are not letting in. That negative emotion always is inflamed when you focus on the fact that they got it, which amplifies your awareness that you do not have it, but if it was not something that you wanted, you would not feel jealousy. *So, it is not about your relationship with them; it is about your relationship within your own vibration—always, every single time.*

There are all kinds of people who have all kinds of things . . . Esther parked the motor coach in Chula Vista [near San Diego] down on the marina, and Esther and Jerry take their walk every day out onto the pier. And Esther has kidded Jerry, over time, and said, "I'm proud to announce to you that I don't want a boat. It's one of the few things I don't want, but I don't want a boat." So it does not matter how beautiful the boats are; they do not ring her bells. She does not find a need or desire for a boat.

The most magnificent boat in the whole world could go by, and Esther would not feel a pang of discomfort about her current status relative to a boat because she *does not want* a boat.

So whenever you feel negative emotion, it is always about your relationship with your own desires, every single time. And they are just helping you, through their exposure to you, understand your vibrational relationship within your own vibration.

That is what you need to clean up.

Guest: Wow, that was helpful.

Abraham Is As Dead As It Gets

Guest: Hi. I've been working the principles for a few years, and everything has gone famously well. Beautiful, beautiful, beautiful. The one tripping point I have that I can't seem to wrap my brain around, and some people seem to be very comfortable with it, is *death*. I'm terrified of death and the notion of death.

Abraham: Well, describe it. What is it?

Guest: It's the loss of consciousness. It's . . .

Abraham: No, it is not! *It is the coming into full Consciousness!* No wonder you fear it. You do not understand what it is. It is not losing focus; it is regaining enormous focus. It is reemerging into the fuller, broader, brighter, surer, happier *you!*

Guest: How do you get a personal knowing about it?

Abraham: Die. Or ask someone who is dead (fun!). We are dead. And we are bright, brilliant, tapped-in-to Infinite Intelligence, joyous, rewarded, creative—and we are as dead as it gets.

Guest: So it's just taking *your* word for it. There's no way to move up the *Vibrational Scale?*

Abraham: Die, and then you will know. You should hear the raucous laughter that happens, especially when several people die at once. Usually what they say is, "Boy, did *I* have it wrong." Usually what they say is, "All that worry for nothing. All of that pinching myself off from the joy of life while I worried about a death that doesn't exist."

When you release your focus from this body, you leave behind all doubt and fear. Talk about a quantum leap! Talk about moving from wherever you are all the way into Pure Positive Energy. Talk about leaving resistance behind and gaining the clarity that comes when you do that! What a whoosh that is!

And for those like Esther, and many of you who are coming every day to move yourself deliberately up the <u>*Emotional Guidance Scale*</u>*— your death experience will just feel like the next logical step.* Esther, who has had the advantage (and others of you, too) of allowing this Source Energy to flow through her for so many hours, for so many days, for so many years, is acclimated to that vibration. So her death experience will just feel like the next logical step. She is not going to feel the enormous relief that someone might who has been vibrating consistently in fear, despair, or even in frustration, you see.

But it does not matter where you have been on the *Emotional Guidance Scale.* When you withdraw focus, you reemerge into that Energy that is really *you.* There will not be a moment's loss of awareness of who you are. You do not become part of a nebulous mist; you do not lose your sense of identity; you do not wonder where you are; you do not feel suffocated for lack of oxygen. You do not miss your body. Instead, you feel all that you have ever been. You have access to go anywhere that you want to go. You can participate in your funeral if you want to. You can reactivate the vibration of your Beingness.

In other words, you could, from your Non-Physical perspective (you call it dead; we like to call it *croaking* to be disrespectful, since there is no such thing as death) reactivate the vibration that was you, and feel as if you were still in your physical body. But you know what? Nobody wants to do that because the broader perspective is so intoxicating.

And then you acclimate and remember who you are, and you make your acquaintances with those whom you have been wondering about as you reemerge into that broader and broader perspective. And one thing that does happen that makes you feel a little insecure from your physical format is that large parts of your human personality are negatively oriented, and *those* will be left behind. So you only take the very best of you with you. But you do not miss the other part.

Often, after a discussion like this, we have to remind you that you wanted very much to be in these bodies. In other words, do not go jumping off buildings. We know that you are going to have that experience when you reemerge into the Non-Physical, but that gate swings both ways. We want you to move up the *Emotional Guidance Scale* so that you have all of that infused in you, here and now, you see. That is what you are here to do. You are here to live, here and now.

You are not here trying to climb the rungs of the ladder or get marks on the chart or to achieve some sort of understanding or perfection so that you can go back and claim a job well done.

You are on the Leading Edge of thought! You are Source Energy, out here on the Leading Edge. And everything that you do and everything that you experience is contributing to the expansion of not just the time-space reality, but *All-That-Is*. This is powerful, this Leading-Edge place.

So we do not want you to necessarily jump into death—but we want you to no longer fear it. And we have never known anyone who could really live their physical life until they leave behind their fear of death, and we think you pretty much just did that. Practice it.

Guest: Okay, thank you.

Abraham Closes Classic Art of Allowing Workshop

Abraham: We think you have it. We do not think that there is anything that we could discuss that would add any stronger points of clarity over any of the things that you are chewing upon. We know that everything that you have come to understand, which you wanted to know, we have addressed in some way, and in many cases, many ways and many times.

We want to say to you that we are all making too much of this . . . that life is supposed to be fun, and that the basis of your life is freedom . . . and that expansion is inevitable . . . and that you are utterly worthy Beings. If you could relax and pet your cat and dangle your feet in the stream and find things that please you and focus upon them . . . and spend time with the people who make you feel best and read the books that make you feel best and go to the movies that make you feel best and take the drives that make you feel best and think of the aspects of those you work with who make you feel best . . . and think of your parents in the way that makes you feel best and make lists of things that you like that make you feel best and wear the clothing that makes you feel best and eat the food that makes you feel best and do the things that make you feel best and think the thoughts that make you feel best . . . hmm, you would feel pretty good.

Life would then begin treating you in the way that you deserve. But when you believe that you are here to overcome struggle, and when you believe that you have things that you have to achieve, and when you believe that you are unworthy and you have to prove worthiness, and when you believe that you are in competition for resources—then you get all distorted and out of sync with who-you-really-are.

We know that many of you have been taught many of those things, and we feel you and we hear you, struggling to try to find your way in all of this. But it is our promise to you that life is supposed to be fun, and that you are worthy without paying any price, and that if you can work to relax just a little bit and work to lighten up just a little bit and try to bring more humor into your experience and try to be more playful with others and let things bother you a little less and be easier about all things and say things to those who surround you (especially your children, your lovers, or your partners) such as, "No big deal." Or, say things to them such as, "Well, isn't that a heck of a thing? What a funny deal that is." Or, say things to them such as, "Why in the world am I making such a big, hairy deal out of something that doesn't mean diddly squat?" In other words, play down the drama and the trauma of everything everywhere you can.

Do not join those groups that want to make more of things than they are. Do not join those groups that have the spotlight shining on the "sewer in Paris." In other words, find the best of where you stand, and exaggerate it as much as you can from where you are, and notice that things will get discernibly better, right away. Then do that again. And then do that again. And then do that again. And then do that again. . . .

There is great love here for you, and for now, we are complete.

ఆ§ఆ§ఆ§ ఏ☞ఏ☞ఏ☞

About the Authors

Excited about the clarity and practicality of the translated word from the Beings who call themselves *Abraham*, **Esther** and **Jerry Hicks** began disclosing their amazing *Abraham* experience to a handful of close business associates in 1986.

Recognizing the practical results being received by themselves and by those persons who were asking meaningful questions regarding finances, bodily conditions, and relationships . . . and then successfully applying Abraham's answers to their own situations—Esther and Jerry made a deliberate decision to allow the Teachings of Abraham to become available to an ever-widening circle of seekers of answers on how to live a better life.

Using their San Antonio, Texas, Conference Center as their base, Esther and Jerry have traveled to approximately 50 cities a year since 1989, presenting interactive *Art of Allowing Workshops* to those leaders who gather to participate in this progressive stream of thought. And although worldwide attention has been given to this philosophy of Well-Being by Leading-Edge thinkers and teachers who have, in turn, incorporated many of Abraham's concepts into their best-selling books, scripts, lectures, and so forth, the primary spread of this material has been from person to person—as individuals begin to discover the value of this form of spiritual practicality in their personal life experiences.

Abraham—a group of obviously evolved Non-Physical teachers—speak their broader perspective through Esther Hicks. And as they speak to our level of comprehension through a series of loving, allowing, brilliant, yet comprehensively simple essays in print and in sound—they guide us to a clear connection with our loving Inner Being, and to uplifting self-empowerment from our Total Self.

The Hickses have now published more than 700 Abraham-Hicks books, cassettes, CDs, videos, DVDs . . . and they may be contacted through their extensive interactive Website at **www.abraham-hicks.com;** or by mail at Abraham-Hicks Publications, P.O. Box 690070, San Antonio, TX 78269.

∙≼∙≼∙≼ ≽∙≽∙≽∙

Hay House Titles of Related Interest

Books

The Disappearance of the Universe,
by Gary R. Renard

How to Get from Where You Are to Where You Want to Be,
by Cheri Huber

I Can Do It®, by Louise L. Hay

If I Can Forgive, So Can You!, by Denise Linn

The Power of Intention, by Dr. Wayne W. Dyer
(also available as a card deck, calendar, and CD program)

Power vs. Force, by David R. Hawkins, M.D., Ph.D.

The Success Book, by John Randolph Price

You Can Have an Amazing Life . . . in Just 60 Days!,
by Dr. John F. Demartini

CD Programs

Igniting Intuition, by Christiane Northrup, M.D.,
and Mona Lisa Schulz, M.D., Ph.D.

Intuitive Power, by Caroline Myss

Letting Go and Becoming, by Marianne Williamson

Karma Releasing, by Doreen Virtue, Ph.D.

·:[▨]:·

All of the above are available at your local bookstore,
or may be ordered through Hay House.

·:[▨]:·